The Entrepreneur's Toolkit: The Ultimate Guide to Building a Multi-million Dollar Business , By Jonathan Newman

First Published in Great Britain by Jonathan Newman

All rights reserved. No part of this book my be reproduced or used in any way or form whatsoever.

Creative Design/Layout:
Kyra Devine

Copyright © 2018 by Jonathan Newman
All rights reserved.

THE ENTREPRENEUR'S TOOLKIT:
THE ULTIMATE GUIDE TO BUILDING A MULTI-MILLION POUND BUSINESS

WRITTEN BY JONATHAN NEWMAN

WHY BUY THIS BOOK?

Chances are, if you've opened this book, you're interested in starting, running or selling a business.

PAT YOURSELF ON THE BACK. YOUR JOURNEY TO A NEW CAREER, AND A NEW LIFE...BEGINS RIGHT NOW.

I've not just the guy that's talking the talk. I'm also the guy that has walked the walk. I've been there and done that.

I was recently at an event discussing my business with a recent MBA graduate who made the comment I knew more than he did after he had just graduated with a business degree. I commented back that you cannot lead an army if you have not been on the frontline yourself.

Whilst this is a lovely ego boost, I'm really telling you this because I'm entirely self-taught. And if I can do it... so can you.

My own journey, as both a business owner and a filmmaker, and also as an individual interested in personal growth, has given me some invaluable skills and an insight that will transform everything you know about success.

WHAT YOU WILL LEARN

This is a guide to building your business from start to finish. From that spark of inspiration, to making it happen, I'll give you practical tips on how to get your business off the ground, how to run it effectively, how not to go out of business, and how to sell it when the time is right.

Along the way, you'll get motivated and inspired and learn some practical business tips, useful formulas, and bits of easily digestible economics.

WHO IS THIS BOOK FOR?

Whilst this book is called The Entrepreneur's Toolkit, it's not just aimed at people who want to start and run a successful business.

It's much more holistic.

And whilst I guarantee you will understand the nuts and bolts of business and entrepreneurship with extremely practical tips they don't teach you at business school, there is a lot more to offer than that which goes way beyond economics, and I encourage you to embrace the entrepreneurial mindset and some of the more out there ideas that I discuss.

BUT DON'T BELIEVE A WORD I SAY. ROAD TEST IT ALL YOURSELF.

This is also aimed at anyone who is 'stuck' in his or her life. This might be stuck in a way of being, stuck in a relationship where things aren't working, stuck in any aspect of your career.

Success is something that anyone can achieve in their life if they want it. I will show you how you can achieve it if you set your mind to it.

Every week, I am approached by someone who wants to 'pick my brain'. Sometimes this is an entrepreneur starting a business. Sometimes this is someone who is a year or two into their business and wants to know how I did it and how they can replicate my success. I am usually willing to sit down and discuss and pass on what I know if it can help. *(note: before you rush out and contact me, nowadays I work on a consultancy fee or equity. Do remember that the best form of currency is reciprocation. After all, you wouldn't walk into a bakery and ask for free bagels, now, would you?)*

This has been a recurring theme for years, whether I am giving a talk on film or a speech on business. I do love helping and inspiring people to reach for and attain their dreams. I believe it's possible for everyone. I do. But I believe that too many people find 'rackets' in their life why they cannot achieve what they wish to achieve. I call these things rackets because they are like excuses we make (whether it be time, money or something else).

WHAT'S STOPPING YOU?

If you have picked up this book just out of interest, I'd like to ask you what is stopping you from achieving your dreams?

You may not know the answer right now… but I can promise that you will come out the other side of this book with more clarity than when you went in.

ARE YOU READY TO CHANGE YOUR LIFE?

TABLE OF CONTENTS

- **THE BIRTH OF CHI**

- **PART 1**

PREFACE: THE 100 MILLION CHEQUE

MAKING YOUR IDEA A REALITY
- The Bright Idea
- Has it been done Before
- Innovation
- Scalability
- Niche Breakouts
- Goods vs Services

BRAND BUILDING
- What is your Brand?
- Registering your Trademark
- What is your product?
- Taking Risks
- Packaging Hierarchy

- **PART 2**

HOW TO RUN AND SUSTAIN A BUSINESS
(AND MAKE MONEY ALONG THE WAY)

FORMING A COMPANY
- Types of Companies
- Companies House

FORMING A BUSINESS PLAN
- What to include in your Business Plan
- EIS Qualifying
- Sample SWOT analysis

MONEY

- Why you need it.
- How to get money / Sources of Funding.
- Managing Money
- Book-keeping
- Xero Accounting
- Invoicing
- Expenses

CASH FLOW

- What is it?
- Why it's important
- How it can destroy you
- Practical solutions for keeping your business running an not running out of money
- Credit Terms with Suppliers
- Letters of Credit
- Invoicing
- Bad Debts
- Credit Insurance
- Overdraft Facility
- Invoice Financing

SIMPLE ECONOMICS EXPLAINED SIMPLY

- Handy Definitions
- Margins Explained
- Getting your Pricing Right (RRPs)
- Five useful formulas every entrepreneur should know
- Pop Quiz
- Reading a Profit & Loss Sheet
- Reading a Balance Sheet

OUTSOURCING

- Time Management
- What is Success?
- Putting together the jigsaw of your business so it can run effortlessly: Checklist

IMPORT/EXPORT
- Trade Fairs
- Consumer Fairs
- HS Codes
- Glossary of Shipping Terms

NETWORKING
- Why you should network.
- Ask and you shall receive.
- Stories of brazen cheek.

GIVING BACK
- Why you should.

THE EXIT PLAN
- Valuing your company
- The £100m Cheque and how to get it, cont'd

TEN GOLDEN RULES OF BUSINESS

TEN GOLDEN RULES OF MAKING YOUR IDEA A REALITY

CASE STUDIES
- Sahar Hashemi – Coffee Republic
- James Averdieck - GÜ
- Peter Granger – CAFÉ POD
- Jo & Seph's

• APPENDIX

SAMPLE BUSINESS PLAN

SAMPLE NEW CUSTOMER/CREDIT FORM

"AND ABOVE ALL, WATCH WITH GLITTERING EYES THE WHOLE WORLD AROUND YOU BECAUSE THE GREATEST SECRETS ARE ALWAYS HIDDEN IN THE MOST UNLIKELY PLACES..." - ROALD DAHL

THE BIRTH OF CHI

chi/kʌi/noun: qi: the circulating life force whose existence and properties are the basis of much Chinese philosophy and medicine.

The Thai Tsunami, 2004
It all started on a beach in Thailand.

Sipping around five young green coconuts a day, I started to feel really great, healthy and energised.

This was 25 December, 2004, and as myself and my wife rode a boat from Phi Phi Island to Krabi, a seismic Tsunami was triggered by an undersea earthquake in the Indian Ocean. We missed the wave by about 5 minutes, but the boat behind us was not so lucky as hoards of tourists arrived at our hotel soaking wet and covered in blood. We spent the next few days aiding with the rescue operation and watching the devastating wreck that is now so well documented.

Some time back in London, around, 2008/9, I discovered coconut water in a little carton. I was amazed that this little drink I loved so much was now available in a shop in London. I started looking into coconut water, it's benefits, and the buzz it was generating. Even celebs like Madonna were getting involved.

I thought to myself, "I can do better than that!" And so, having no experience whatsoever in retail, branding or manufacturing, I set in motion the insane plan to launch my own coconut water.

Where do you start when you have nothing?

No product, no brand, no connections? It's almost so monumental as to be overwhelming, and that 'fear' (more on fears later), is enough to stop you from even getting off the ground.

With £200 I hired a freelance designer and the first designs for what was then "Yococo" were born. I managed to find a few suppliers in Thailand to send me samples, made a presentation and then went to see a big distributor.

THE FUNDRAISE

"Jonathan," they said, *"you really need a minimum of £500,000 to start a brand. But, if you had that, we'd be interested in distributing your brand."*

"Give me 3 months," I said, *"I will raise the money and be back."*

I firmly believed, with every fibre of my body, that I would be able to raise the money (more on the law of attraction later). Even though I was not sure *how* I was going to raise the money, I set about on my journey.

I pitched at angel's dens, Googled everything and everyone, and left no stone unturned. I had no idea what a profit and loss sheet looked like but, nonetheless, I made one along with a business plan. I met curmudgeonly old men who had sold their businesses - who grilled me for weeks only to fizzle out into nothing leaving me with the bill for lunch. I had meeting after meeting. I fielded questions about margins, profit, EBITDA, and a whole host of things that meant nothing to me... somehow blagging my way through. I remained totally passionate about the product itself.

I finally cobbled together £200k through friends of friends and the company was finally formed. Little did I know that someone else had just registered "Gococo". This was actually a blessing in disguise for me.

Being so similar, I decided to change the brand and tried to think of something that didn't have the word 'coco' in the name, that could encompass a range of products if I ever decided to extend the range. I settled on CHI, because I felt it perfectly and harmoniously signified the energy and definition of what coconut water was in 3 simple letters. One of my models here was GU, launched by my now good friend James Averdieck. What I liked about GU was that it didn't define or limit the product, but instead captured the essence of the brand's spirit.

Coconut water, if you don't know, has been used for centuries in tropical countries. It is packed with electrolyte minerals such as potassium, calcium, magnesium, and phosphorous. These minerals regulate and hydrate the body and the blood PH. In fact, in many developing countries, coconut water, because it is sterile within the coconut, is used as an alternative to medical saline solution and injected intravenously.

It was, perhaps, late 2011, early 2012 when CHI launched into Planet Organic and Wholefoods to start with. It was always my goal to start with the highest quality raw material.

We were late to the market, which really scared me, but I knew we had a kick ass brand, amazing branding, and a great quality product. I was proud of what I had created.

I ran CHI by myself for over a year from the loft of my house, simultaneously shooting two feature films. It was nuts. We nearly went out of business in the first year because a customer in Australia didn't pay us and then copied our branding and changed the name, opening a whole legal Pandora's box. It was a steep learning curve. I got through it through perseverance, and after that hurdle, CHI started going from strength to strength.

Next, I launched some fruit flavoured coconut waters, mixed with mango, pineapple and tropical fruit juices. This was followed by some dairy free milks made from coconut milk - one yummy chocolate and another with espresso coffee. My ethos was always to remain healthy and delicious, never use preservatives or anything artificial, and to go organic when we could. I did not have interest in peddling a sub-standard product. Integrity is ultimately more interesting than money (not to everyone). But start with integrity, and you'll reap the benefits of a successful high quality product as consumers discover it for themselves.

We then launched our raw organic coconut oil - amazing for cooking, moisturizing or spreading, and our 1 litre coconut milk, perfect as a natural milk alternative.

In 2015 I was able to finally launch my favourite product, our raw, organic coconut water. It's made from 6 month old Nam-Hom coconuts harvested at their peak. Totally fresh and unpasteurised, it's bottled the same day the coconuts are received and cut open. We use a cutting edge technology called HPP (High Pressure Processing), which exerts 60,000 tons of pressure on the bottle at a cold temperature. This amazing technology reduces the bacteria to a safe micro level suitable for consumption. The nutritional enzymes and taste are completely intact. If it were champagne it would be a Moet. It truly is incredible and I urge you to try it if you have not done so. If you are lucky enough to get a pink one, (nature's way of blushing), it's because the phenols in the anti-oxidants react to light, and is a natural phenomenon of raw coconut water that has not been messed about with or pasteurised.

At the time of writing we are launching a fantastic coconut oil pulling product, which whitens teeth and removes plaque and bacteria.

I'm also very proud to have launched a snack range called The Giving Tree, which is freeze dried fruit and vegetable crisps. These are amazing because the moisture is removed, but 100% of the nutritional content is preserved naturally along with the fibre. They are a delicious and nutritious snack and 1 of your 5 a day too.

You can see I'm really passionate about my products. I couldn't do something I'm not passionate about. Could you? Well, the truth is, a lot of (most of the population) do.

Finally, we are really proud of our continued partnership with Drop4Drop.org. Every year we build 6 wells in underdeveloped communities in India and Africa, thanks to the hard work of Simon and Lucas who run the charity and look forward to continuing this important collaboration.

At the time of writing, CHI is in over 30 countries and thousands of stores in the UK including all the major supermarkets like Waitrose, Tesco and Asda. Not bad for a brand that launched 4 years ago by a filmmaking guy with no retail experience at all.

That's not to say I didn't make mistakes along the way. In fact, I made many. And most of what I know is from the mistakes I have made.

That's why I've written this book for you. It won't stop you making your own mistakes and, in fact, I encourage you to make mistakes. Failure is how we grow and learn.

Just consider this book like a little road map, or an A-Z (for you youngsters, an A-Z was a map of London before we had sat-nav and iphones!). You'll find it easier to get from North London to South London if you know where you're going.

CHI PRODUCTS

GIVING TREE RANGE

PART 1

MAKING YOUR IDEA A REALITY

PREFACE: THE £100 MILLION CHEQUE

As a writer, I can tell you that knowing the end of the story does not take away from the enjoyment of the journey itself.

If anything, it makes it more interesting.

So, like many great films I have seen, I want to start with the end. And a little secret...

Here it is...

Last year, I wrote a cheque to myself for 100 million pounds.

In fact, here is a picture of the cheque, currently on my fridge held up by some magnets:

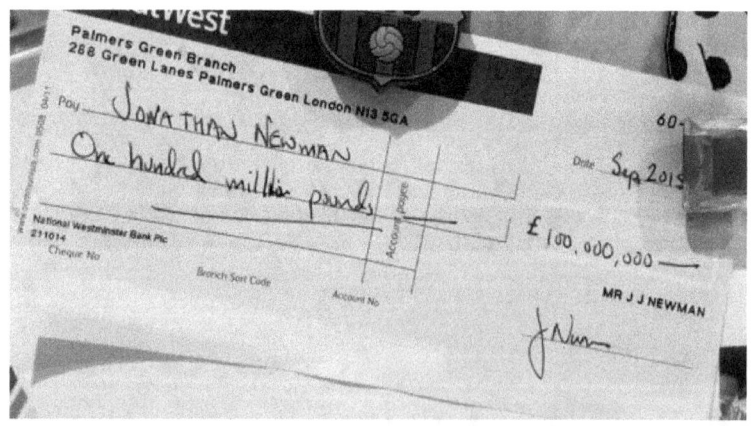

I realize, to the average person, this might sound crazy. It almost sounds crazy to me too.

But that's what I did. I wrote a cheque for £100m to myself.

I cannot tell you anymore than this for now.

I'm so sorry to tease you.

I know you want to know. But you'll have to wait and watch the rest of the movie.

So, before I tell you about this £100m cheque, the secret to running a business, and the meaning of life, please get some popcorn, put your feet up and enjoy the trailers followed by the main feature.

HOW TO MANIFEST ANYTHING YOU WANT IN YOUR LIFE

Before I get on to the business side of being an entrepreneur, you need to sort yourself out.

You really do.

You need to sort out your mind, your attitude, your approach to life, and your approach to success and to failure.

There is a veil in between your sight and that which is real. It's like the movie the Matrix. Life will always present you with choices – the red pill or the blue pill. And it's up to you which you take and what doors open up for you along the way.

DON'T SKIP THIS.

This is the stuff that will separate you from the average Joe. This is the material that will help you grow as a person and, consequently, manifest success in your business, your life, your relationships and any area you feel stuck.

It's the reason I succeeded (though failure is always just a bus stop away from success). It's a mindset I use everyday in my life – whether it's making a phone call to a customer to chase money, or in my personal life when I am upset, angry or depressed.

And it has little to do with luck or even business acumen - though these forces do have *some* bearing on success.

You might question what place does all this psychology have being in a book about building a business or being an entrepreneur.

Everything. Because successful businesses are build by successful people.

Successful entrepreneurs share many similar traits: the ability to pick themselves up after failure, persistence, not being stopped by fears... just to name a few.

Therefore if you REALLY want to succeed as an entrepreneur you need to embrace the mindset of the entrepreneur, or at least be conscious of the journey you will face and the internal struggle that inevitably awaits you.

Even Olympic athletes still need a coach to help win the gold. It's not unreasonable, then, to open your mind to the possibility of continued self growth.

Imagine you are the athlete, and I am your coach, willing you to win gold.

Your marathon begins now. Remember this race is not against anyone else. It's your own race and you'll finish in your own time.

Good luck. And I hope to see you at the finish line.

THE PIE CHART OF YOUR LIFE

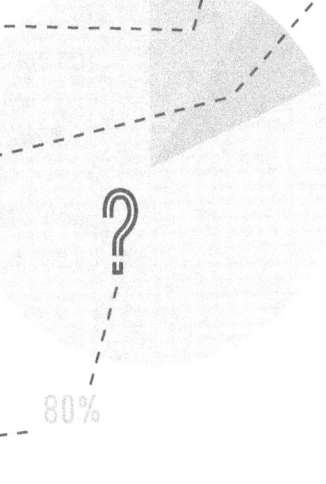

THINGS YOU KNOW YOU KNOW
There are things you know you know. For example, you know how to ride a bicycle, and you know how to send email.

THINGS YOU KNOW YOU DON'T KNOW
There are things you know you don't know. For example, you know you don't know Russian. Or you know you don't how about quantum particle physics (unless you are a particle physicist of course).

THINGS YOU DON'T KNOW YOU DON'T KNOW
Consider that when you drive a car, you have a blind spot in your

vision. There are spots that none of the mirrors can see. As a result, there are things happening in those blind spots that you have no awareness of. Because you can't see it, it doesn't exist in your realm of what is. You are existing in the small slivers of what you know you know and what you know you don't know.

Imagine for a moment that you were born into an imprisoned room with no windows and no doors. You were fed through a small trap in the wall. If this were your life, this is all you would know. You know there is food, but you don't know how it is made or where it comes from. Now imagine that one day you were set free, and you discovered trees, animals, lakes, countries, airplanes, and computers. Suddenly an incredible world expands your knowledge of what is, whereas before, all you knew was the room.

From what you don't know that you don't know, the biggest transformation will occur in your life.

In order to access this transformation in your life, you will need to lower your wall, and allow for the possibility that there is something more than what currently is.

All invention in the world tends to come from the things we don't know we don't know.

The unanswered questions about space, the universe, black holes and quantum physics are buried in the realm of what we don't yet know we don't know. Before there was any knowledge that electricity existed, there was simply light and darkness, and all people knew were that electric fish could create shocks (true fact by the way, look it up!).

Similarly, there was no knowledge of anything remotely resembling a light bulb. All we had were candles.

True invention comes from what we don't know we don't know.

Even the idea of the creation of life and the universe are questions we cannot answer today, because there are so many mysteries to the universe that are beyond the realm of our knowledge. We can hypothesize, but it is like putting together a jigsaw puzzle when you do not even have the pieces to start with.

THE THEORY OF CONNECTIVITY

In the 1990s, Masaru Emoto [1], a Japanese researcher, conducted a series of experiments on how human thoughts and consciousness have the power to effect water molecules. In possibly the most famous of these experiments, Emoto filled 3 cups of water and spoke to each cup for a month. To the first cup he professed his love, the other his hate, and the third he ignored. By the end of the experiment, Emoto claimed that under microscopic examination, the molecular structure of the water and crystal formations had radically altered – each relative in beauty, smell and sensory formation to that of the words spoken (the experiments can be found on YouTube and also in the movie "What the "Bleep" do we Know").

Similarly, we know from a quantum physics test called the "Double Slit Experiment [2]," that the very act of observing the experiment can alter the actual outcome of the experiment and, hence, the molecular structure of everything in that room. Wow. Imagine if you could use THAT magic in a business meeting to alter the outcome to your advantage?

Would you try if you knew you could?

Quantum physics tells us that there is no such thing as solid mass. Every molecule and every atom is constantly in flux and interconnected, and when other atoms are present, seismic changes can occur to alter those atoms.

The biggest take away is how our thoughts and feelings can

influence those around us and, indeed, ourselves. Think about how we talk to children, or how our internal anger or sadness has the power to affect loved ones in our lives, or even ourselves. Fill your cup with anger, and anger will pour from it. Fill your cup with love, and love will pour from it.

Think about how dwelling on the past or a tragic event can create sadness in your life, and ultimately alter your physical health.

Think about how one's perception of one's body (ultimately merely a thought created by our mind), can manifest in an eating disorder such as anorexia or bulimia. The internal, mental stream of consciousness manifests in reality in the actions we take and the choices we make.

> CONSCIOUSNESS OCCURS IN THAT MOMENT WHEN YOU FEEL REACTIVE.

The difference between happy and sad is as simple as what we choose to feel. Think happy thoughts and you will be happy. (read my chapter later on 'SMILING')

At this point you might be thinking that sometimes we don't have a choice about how we feel. I put it to you that this is the only thing we do have control of. We are unable to control other people and how they are. We cannot control how they interpret our actions, how they react to us, how they feel internally and how they express themselves. But we can alter the way we are towards them. Simply choosing to give up our `story' of events (more on this shortly), and choosing a different scenario can radically alter the moment and, hence, the outcome. Alter the way you are to others, find out how you have been inauthentic in the relationship (even if you adamantly believe you have not been). The key is to then express this in language to the person, and that person will then alter the way they are to you.

Imagine in the worst scenario possible, that someone killed your child. They were caught and went to prison for life. Naturally, you grieve. But 5 years later your life is still a wreck. Your choice, here, is to remain in your virtual fortress of solitude, left with anger, sadness and hatred for the rest of your foreseeable future. You lock yourself in your house and never go out. You cut yourself off from the world, your friends, and your partner. Your relationships crumble. Your marriage breaks down.

Though not in a physical prison you are in a mental one, but the mental prison has walls that can be broken down through thought and conscious choice. The memory of the past, haunts your present and your future. You live today based on an event that happened 5 years ago.

This doesn't mean there is no place for emotions or feelings. Bad things happen in our lives. And it's normal to react, to feel and to emote relative to that situation. And you should. The distinction here is how quickly you are able to take that event and place it in the past. This doesn't mean forget about the memory. Memories shape our lives. But holding onto emotions, especially negative emotions, that are associated with *past* events... *dominates* our *present*. As a result they do not allow us to live in the present free from the past. We are shackled by how an event made us feel a year ago, or when we were a child. We relive that past emotion in the present day, and we allow it to imprison our future choices.

Consciousness occurs in that moment when you feel reactive. Resisting the urge to react, pausing, and waiting can often provide a different solution to that of the reactive, emotive one.

This is something you can try out in business. Next time you get an email or a phone call that really winds you up, do not respond straight away.

Your initial response comes from a place of emotion. It is only through this 'restriction' of response, that you will find clarity above and beyond the immediate emotional response. So next time you get that email... try not sending that angry response back straight away. Save it. Come back it the next day, and see if you feel the same way. I'll wager a bet that you'll have thought of a different, more proactive way to handle the situation.

SUPERNOVAS & STAR STUFF

"We are a way for the universe to know itself. Some part of our being knows this is where we came from. We long to return. And we can, because the cosmos is also within us. We're made of star stuff," –Carl Sagan

A number of scientific studies have concluded that everything on earth contains minuscule carbon particles originating from stars. A combination of carbon, nitrogen and oxygen atoms in our bodies created over 4.5 billion years ago during the explosion of a massive star, called a Supernova. On a basic quantum level, if this theory is to be considered, all the matter in the universe and all of the people in it are, essentially, made up of the same connected stardust.

If this is the case, we work very hard, as a species, at working for the self, as opposed to the collective, much to our own peril and self-destruction.

THINK OF AN ANT COLONY.

Amazingly, one ant can move up to 50 times it's own body weight. That means that 10 ants working together can carry up to 500 times their own collective weight. We've all seen the amazing videos on Youtube of an ant collective moving seemingly impossibly large objects together as a group. They work together, with an ant captain and ant guides, to move large objects to their nest.

Yet the human species, for the most part, insists on working just for the benefit of the self. Think how much more we could accomplish as a collective, working together as a universal whole to move mountains if we realised we are all on the same earth, and we are all, ultimately, connected.

Sometimes we do, and when we do we get it right – like coming together to help the current Syrian refugee crisis, or the creation of the UN to come to global solutions to world issues, or coming together for Comic Relief, or Bob Geldof's charity single "We are the World." And when you are a part of that global connectivity, you can move seismic objects 500 times your weight.

But the reason we often don't work together, as the most advanced of the species on our planet, is because of something called the 'ego'. The ego tricks us into believing that we are the centre of the universe.

When it rains, we think it is ruining our day. In fact, it is raining everywhere and ruining everyone's day.

On a global level, wars are generally fought by individuals whose story of the way the world is dominates their reality. They fail to see the connectivity of human beings, instead focussing on the self, or the idea that their personal glorification will come in the afterlife if they pick up arms and kill off all infidels. They fill their cup with hatred, anger and murder, blindly following the interpretation of a script they believe to be reality. This is the cause, and the effect is death. If there is one thing that history has shown, it is that one act of killing in the name of culture or civilisation, creates an opposite but equal reaction of war. And the cycle continues.

As civilised human beings, it is quite remarkable, but not entirely surprising, that we have not, as a species, been unable to overcome our desire for self-destruction. As the most intelligent of species on the planet, it appears we are the *only* species that consistently and consciously chooses paths that will extinguish our life.

Whilst on the one hand, we have become more technologically advanced, we have remained somewhat stunted in our personal, inner transformative growth. Even now, wars around the world show no signs of abating. The current political climate in the Middle East with Syria, ISIS, and other political factions, has groups of people attempting to extinguish entire populations of people (the Yazidis for example, or the Christians or the Jews). After the Holocaust during WW2, the sentiment was "never forget". Whilst we may have not forgotten, we are almost powerless to stop our own civilisation from self-destruction. We treat the cause of the self-destructive population, with more self-destruction, and so the cycle of endless destruction continues.

Whilst this might seem like a bleak outlook on life and, perhaps, a digression, and you might read this feeling powerless to control any of it:

...the best place to start, for now, is with you.

Control what you do have power over. Indeed, one day you might be in a position of political power, and if you are enlightened enough (perhaps after having read this book ;-), and have control over your own consciousness, you may be able to exert the idea of 'casuality' (cause and effect) on the global landscape of politics.

CAUSE & EFFECT

It is easy to go through life thinking we are a victim of circumstance. Things happen TO us, right? A relationship crumbles, a partner cheats, a friendship breaks up, you get fired from a job. We convince ourselves that the world is conspiring *against* us, and we are merely the *recipients* of bad tidings.

Cause and effect is, fundamentally, a scientific principle. Newton's 3rd Law: **FOR EVERY ACTION THERE IS AN EQUAL AND OPPOSITE REACTION.**

For every interaction, there is a pair of forces acting on the two interacting objects. Both forces are opposite and the size of the force on the object equals the size of the opposite force.

This principle is evident throughout our natural environment. Consider a fish that swims through water using its fins to push backwards. The force of the action of its fins causes a force on the water, which, in turn, accelerates the fish's movement to move forwards.

The same applies to the idea of birds in flight. Whilst the force of the wings pushes against the air downwards, the force on the air allows the bird to propel forwards.

AND AS WELL AS AN EQUAL FORCE IN SIZE, THERE IS AN EQUAL FORCE IN THE OPPOSITE DIRECTION.

Cause and effect formed one of Aristotle's main philosophies and is also one of the central tenets of Buddhism and also Kabbalah.

CAUSALITY IS ALSO KNOWN AS KARMA, IE WHAT GOES AROUND COMES AROUND

The general idea is that everything that happens to us is because of a seed we planted, perhaps unconsciously, and even years and years ago.

Imagine you just got fired.

On a subconscious level, perhaps you hated your work. This, in turn, lowered your productivity and also affected your attitude towards your colleagues and your boss. So when you finally did get fired, was it really that much of a surprise and was it really without any of your own making?

ACTION IS DRIVEN

AND EVENTUALLY

CONSEQUENCES,

FAR **DOWN**

(BUDDHISM WOULD EVEN
SAY THESE SEEDS   ARE

BY INTENTION

LEADS TO FUTURE

NO MATTER HOW

THE LINE...

PLANTED IN PAST LIVES).

Cause and effect can be both negative and positive. Fill your cup with love, and love will pour out of your cup. Fill your cup with hatred, and hatred will pour out.

IN THE PHILOSOPHICAL SENSE, THE IDEA HERE IS TO PLANT POSITIVE SEEDS FOR FUTURE GROWTH.

Likewise, acknowledge you are the maker of your destiny, rather than shifting the blame to 'them" (ie everyone else). By planting positive seeds now, with no immediate expectation of return, the seeds will germinate, grow, and eventually flower into something beautiful in your life. Up from the ashes grow the roses of success.

You are on a severely congested road. Both sides converge in the middle and no cars can get through – it's gridlock. You beep. The cars facing you beep. It's a standoff and no one is moving (like the Dr Seuss story the Zax – where the North Going Zax and the South going Zax meet and neither move!). Driven by your desire to 'get there first' and based on the idea of 'just you', your ego has created gridlock, frustration, and anger – for you and for all those behind and in front of you. All it will actually take to get through is for one car to reverse, but our indignant need to be right, stops us from being the one to give in. In this instance, whilst all we might be thinking about is ourselves, we are all intrinsically connected. Had we not driven up the road in the first place and waited for the traffic to come though, everyone would have gotten through in good time. Had we thought of the 'whole' as opposed to the 'component', both the component and the collective group would have been better off. Had you been able to see the road from a bird's eye perspective would you still have driven down it? Knowing that your action would cause gridlock, but your staying still would allow all to pass through?

CONSIDER THIS.

You are in a dark church hall with a large group of people. You are the only person holding a lit candle. You want to hold onto your candle, because you think that if you give it away, you won't have any more light and will not be able see.

However, by lighting everyone else's candle, not only is your candle still lit, but now everyone's is lit, and not only can you see better, but the entire church hall can see better than before.

The simple act of *giving* away light, rather than hoarding it for yourself, actually brought you more light and had the consequential effect of transforming those around you as well. And you now feel great about yourself because you've just helped out everyone around you.

Sometimes, the act of giving, allows you to receive more of what you actually want.

GREED AND WHY IT'S NOT GOOD.

"The point is, ladies and gentleman, that greed – for lack of a better word – is good. Greed is right. Greed works. Greed clarifies, cuts through, and captures the essence of the evolutionary spirit. Greed, in all of its forms – greed for life, for money, for love, knowledge – has marked the upward surge of mankind. And greed – you mark my words – will not only save Teldar Paper, but that other malfunctioning corporation called the USA."
– Gordon Gecko, WALL STREET (the movie)

Whilst a very convincing and seductive monologue delivered with aplomb by Michael Douglas, greed is what destroyed the banks, the mortgage markets, brought down many economies, large businesses, governments and has split families.

At the second International Conference on Nutrition (CIN2) in Rome in 2014, Pope Francis warned:

'GOD ALWAYS FORGIVES, BUT THE EARTH DOES NOT.'

Whether greed in a corporation, or greed on a personal level, greed might bring you some temporary joy, but there is no lasting joy to be had in greed.

LIGHT

In fact, the need for us, as humans, to hold onto as much light as we possibly can, is so incredibly strong, that we have virtually all but lost the ability to give away our light. There is nothing inherently wrong with receiving light, but without the balance of giving away light, you cannot reach true spiritual happiness or transformation.

It's the Oscars. It comes around once a year and you love watching the show. It's your favouite show. You are just about to sit down and watch it when your son comes up to you and says

"DAD, WILL YOU PLAY FOOTBALL WITH ME?"
"BUT... IT'S THE OSCARS! I CAN'T, SON, IT'S ONLY ONCE A YEAR."
"BUT DAD, YOU NEVER PLAY WITH ME - AND I'D LOVE TO PLAY BALL WITH YOU."

You have a choice here. Fulfill your own need to watch television (which, after all, is a very temporary moment of satisfaction), or play ball. A small voice inside tells you the right thing to do is probably switch off the TV and play with your son, even though you LOVE the Oscars! Reluctantly, you switch off the TV and go play ball.

At the end of the night, though you've completely missed the Oscars, but you've played, smiled, laughed and bonded with your child. Your son turns to you and says, "Dad, this has been one of the best nights ever." A little wave of deep seated happiness ripples through your body and you smile. By giving away your light, you have received even more light than you could have imagined or expected. Not just that, it's the kind of light the lasts forever, because the memories and feelings you have given to your child resonate and shape him as a human being for the rest of his life. The other light of receiving (in this case TV) for the sake of serving the self, is purely temporary.

The distinction here is between pleasure vs happiness. We seek pleasure in things such as cars, money, sex, vacations, etc, and these things give us temporary pleasure. These exist in the realm of our 1% world – a world based on our 5 senses. These things tend to come and go (more often going than coming). And each time they go we seek more. That is why some people get addicted to vices – sex, drugs, shopping etc. Their five sense get momentary pleasure from the act, and strive to be in a continuous state of pleasure by abusing or using that particular vice. And when you are not using, you feel a profound sense of displeasure. It is the mind's way of tricking you into thinking that pleasure can be sustained by reuse or abuse.

Again, on balance, there is nothing wrong with receiving pleasure, no matter how temporary, and I am not suggesting you shave your head and become a Buddhist monk and go live in a cave or give away all your earthly possessions or money to charity.

THE IDEA IS TO BE AWARE OF THE LIGHT AND TO APPRECIATE IT. AND IN SO DOING, MORE LIGHT WILL BE REVEALED.

It is no wonder that so many people, on their deathbed, make the profound realisation that they cannot take their riches, wealth, cars or houses with them. They declare their regrets for not loving enough, for not spending enough time with their partner or children, for unfilled dreams. And they declare their profound love for those around them. This is pure connection to the light, pure awareness and consciousness working from this 99% world.

The path to long lasting spiritual transformation can be found through making choices that involve giving away your own light, even if the reason is because you know you will receive more light of your own by doing so. After all, giving without acknowledgement is no easy feat. The ego demands recognition for the act of giving, because recognition feeds the ego. The act of giving and/or helping anonymously, will ultimately, on a karmic level, bring you even more light.

If temporary pleasure can be found in this 1% world, then true lavorent can be found in the 99% world which is everything else. Before you begin to think that you do not have access to this 99% world, let me tell you that we all do, and we have all accessed it, even if fleetingly so. Think about a perfecting an essay and the sense of pride you feel when you've finished. Or a moment of happiness when you walk through a park and see a beautiful bed of roses, or the love you feel for a child when they open their presents. Or praise from a boss or a co-worker. These are all moments when you have accessed the light. The key now is to figure out how to access it more often.

The light is always every present. Just like the sun. When it gets dark, the sun has not gone anywhere. The earth has simply rotated around it. The sun is there, on the other side of the earth, shining quite bright. There is just a veil between us and it that stops us from seeing it. That veil is the ego.

If something happens to you, you are reacting in this 1% world. If you are happening to that something, you are existing in that 99% world. If the 1% world is the effects, the 99% world is the cause. Imagine you are sick and you have a cold. You keep treating the symptoms of that cold but not the underlying cause. You take medicine to clear your congestion, or a pill to get rid of your headache. When in fact the cause is your weak immune system. So instead you start to exercise, eat better, you are stronger and you get less colds.

To give, you need to be the cause – you need to be proactive, rather than reactive. Giving or sharing takes many forms. We are not just talking about giving money to a charity. Think about the concept of sharing – sharing a secret, or helping an old lady to carry her groceries. Are you sharing when you're having sex? Are you sharing when you have friends round for dinner?

THE LAW OF ATTRACTION

The trouble is in the mind, for the body is only the house for the mind to dwell in, and we put a value on it according to its worth. Therefore if your mind has been deceived by some invisible enemy into a belief, you have put it into the form of a disease, with or without your knowledge. By my theory or truth I come in contact with your enemy, and restore you to your health and happiness. This I do partly mentally and partly by talking till I correct the wrong impressions and establish the Truth, and the Truth is the cure."
– Phineus Quimby

You may be familiar with this concept from the book and movie "The Secret", but the law of attraction is actually an old concept from the 19th Century.

There is nothing mystical about this concept. If you want something hard enough, and you think about that thing and visualise it, thought leads to action, action leads to opportunity and when you seize that opportunity, you manifest your thoughts.

THE POWER OF VISUALISATION

THE LAW OF ATTRACTION AND THE POWER OF VISUALIZATION ARE INTRINSICALLY LINKED.

The power of visualizing what you want in your life is not a mystical or a magical potion that requires spells or Harry Potter to help materialize. And though it might sound rather new age and hippie, it's founded more in the psychology and complexity of the human mind.

In fact, the truth is *buried* there.

STEPS TO MATERIALIZE WHAT YOU DESIRE

Think it.

Write it down on a piece of paper.

Say it. Say it again. And tell everyone. Believe with absolute certainty that you will get it.
Take action consistent with your spoken word
When opportunity presents itself with an open door, which it will, you must walk through it.

The psychology of why this works is as follows.

THOUGHT LEADS TO INTENT

INTENT LEADS TO ACTION

ACTION LEADS TO OPPORTUNITY

OPPORTUNITY LEADS TO RESULTS

And it really is as simple as that.

THOUGHT LEADS TO INTENT. INTENT LEADS TO ACTION. ACTION LEADS TO OPPORTUNITY. OPPORTUNITY LEADS TO RESULTS.

It's as simple as thinking it, to start with. But thinking it is pointless unless you take the other steps in the equation.

Because I live this concept every day, I want to give you a quick example based on the genesis of this book.

Books are enormously and notoriously difficult to publish. In fact, most publishers will tell you that they will not consider unsolicited material unless it is submitted through an agent.

I had the idea for this book about a year ago. Knowing the difficult journey I had ahead of me to get this book published might have been enough to stop me in my very tracks.

But because I believed, with absolute certainty, that I could get this book published, I was convinced I could make it work.

Here's how I did it.

I THOUGHT OF THE IDEA TO WRITE THIS BOOK.
I WROTE THE PROPOSAL FOR THE BOOK
I TOLD ALL MY STAFF I WAS GOING TO WRITE A BOOK AND SHARED MY PROPOSAL, CREATING A REALITY IN LANGUAGE. I BELIEVED IT.
I TOOK ACTION. THIS TOOK TWO FORMS, CONTACTING PEOPLE I KNEW WHO HAD WRITTEN BOOKS, AND ALSO COLD CALLING A FEW PUBLISHERS AS WELL.
TWO DOORS OPENED, HOWEVER I DECIDED TO SELF-PUBLISH.

This simplified explanation makes it sound like it was a fairly simple process for me.

But I must say, along the way, there were some hurdles, and you must be aware of these, because the hurdles are like road blocks which can easily stop you if you are not looking out for them..

For example, a good friend of mine kindly introduced me to her publisher. I duly wrote to the publisher and was met with complete silence. After some persistence, I received a response. They were interested and asked for more info.

I sent more info, got an immediate response but then silence again. I sent a few more emails but heard nothing back. I actually thought the project might be dead in the water with this particular publisher.

I let it rest. I was still running a business and had plenty on my plate and writing a book was a bonus for me.

In fact, a full nine months passed until I made the conscious choice to do it again, recognizing the temporary toad block in my path.

I wrote back to the same publisher, who told me that the woman in question had gone on maternity leave. I managed to resubmit the project and hoped it would get looked at. At the same time, I managed to contact a second publisher through another friend I knew who had written a book.

I also tried a few agents as well, knowing that agents tend to have the relationships with the publishers.

Here is one response I received back from a well known literary agency many weeks after submitting my proposal:

"Dear Jonathan,

Thank you for sending us The Entrepreneur's Toolkit and for giving us the opportunity to consider your work.

JUST A COINCIDENCE?

While we enjoyed reading your submission, which stood out from the many we receive, we couldn't find an agent here who felt strongly enough to take it further and therefore we are afraid we are not able to offer you representation for this project.

Thank you for giving us the opportunity to consider your material and we wish you every success with your writing."

It was quite poetic justice that I had just been made, not one, but two offers from publishers, and you can imagine what I wanted to write back and say just to rub it in their face (just remember karma is a bitch and will come back to bite you one day so that's not advisable!).

Along the way I faced barriers, rejections and silence. I did not stop, nor did I give up. Nor did I let my own doubt or insecurity dominate the conversation.

THESE ARE ALL TEMPORARY ROADBLOCKS DESIGNED TO TEST YOU.

Simultaneously, we are writing a cookbook for my company CHI. I reached out to three publishers – none of which I knew, had any connection with, or even had contact details of. All three publishers have gotten back to me and expressed interest in our cookbook.

Sometimes luck does play a part. And so does opportunity (more on this shortly). But neither of these forces act independently of one another.

I want to give you another example.

Last year my wife and I went to see a house. We fell in love with it. We dawdled a bit and then when we finally went back to make an offer, someone else had beat us to it. They took the house off the market.

We felt slightly gutted. And the more we thought about it, the more we wanted it.

"Shall we visualize it?" I said.

And so we did. We printed out a collage of pictures of the property and the rooms and we stuck it on the fridge where we could see it everyday.

I then called the agent and planted a seed.

"Look," I said. "If anything ever happens with that property please give me a call."

About 3 weeks later, completely out of the blue the agent called me and told me the house was back on the market and did we want it?! In the end we actually turned it down, ironically... but we careful what you wish for...

Cynics out there will be saying this is just coincidence. Or luck.

And you might well be right.

But it's not the first time it's happened to me.

Have you ever thought of someone and then they've called? For me, whenever I think of my good friend Harry, he calls about five minutes later. Has that happened to you?

IS THIS JUST A COINCIDENCE?

And there are plenty of things in the world I will never understand, like how radio waves work, or how my voice travels through my mobile phone and ends up on yours, or the secrets of the universe, or if there is a God. But there are plenty of things I just accept, even if I don't know how they work. I watch TV not understanding how it works or ends up on the panel on my wall, but I accept it.

So could it be possible... if we are all made of star stuff, if we are all interconnected, if our thoughts and feelings can influence the atoms of water molecules... if it is possible, as the quantifiable and scientific proven "Double Slit Experiment suggests," that the mere act of being an observer in a room can alter the outcome of the atoms in that room...

If all *that* is possible...

COULD IT BE POSSIBLE THAT WHAT WE VISUALIZE, THINK, OR DREAM COULD ALTER THE ATOMS IN OUR OWN LIVES TO SHAPE OUR FUTURE?

THE COSMIC DOORS OF OPPORTUNITY

After you have thought about what you want, verbalized it in language and written it down, doors of opportunity will present themselves.

THEY JUST WILL.

You can call it 'coincidence' if you prefer something less mystical, but whatever you call it, it's up to you to be conscious of the opportunity when it arises.

Let's say one of your dreams has always been to be a professional chef. You know you're an amazing cook but it's your dream to give up your job in banking and go full time. You decide this is what you will do. You tell your partner you're going to give up work and become a professional chef.

A few weeks later you are invited to a party and you get to chatting to the person next to you who asks you what you do. You tell them, "Well, I'm in banking, but recently I had an epiphany. I've decided to follow my heart full time and become a chef."

"That's amazing. My friend owns a restaurant and they are looking for a new chef."

Are you conscious of these types of 'coincidences' that happen in your life? I will bet they happen all the time, but if you are not conscious of looking out for them, you will miss them like that blind spot in your car mirror.

These coincidences are like doors that open in cosmic fabric of the universe.

They appear, apparently randomly (are they really random though?!) and often when you least expect them to appear. They remain ajar for a moment in space in time, waiting for you to push them fully open.

YOU ARE FACED WITH A TEMPORARY CHOICE.

Do you push the door open, or does it close and vanish in a puff of smoke.

Most of us miss these doors because we are simply just not looking out for them. Or, we notice them, but we are too afraid or insecure to push them open.

The great thing about doors of opportunity is that you don't always have to wait for them to come to you. You have the power to create them too.

This is the difference between the reactive nature and proactive nature (more on that later).

I create doors of opportunity for myself in my life all the time. I plant many seeds. Some of them I water more than others, and eventually I find one of them has grown into a door that is slightly ajar. And then I push the door open.

Reaching out to publishers for my CHI cookbook, for example – those are seeds that I am planting which I hope will flower into an open door.

My entire filmmaking career was created out of seeds that I planted and doors that opened as a result of my seed sowing. The act of doing one thing inevitably leads to another.

So in case you forgot it already:

THOUGHT LEADS TO INTENT.
INTENT LEADS TO ACTION.
ACTION LEADS TO OPPORTUNITY.
OPPORTUNITY LEADS TO RESULTS.

And if you speak to most entrepreneurs, I bet you will discover they all have one thing in common...

HOW TO MILK THE COW

If you are in a field and you have been asked to milk the cow, do you stand at the edge of the field and wait for the cow to back into your hands?

Or do you walk into the field, go up to the cow, and milk it?

You'd be surprised that most people stand on the edges, waiting for the cow to back into their hands. Waiting for some day, one day – and possibly never.

The odds of a cow backing into your hands are slim. It can happen, but why wait when you can control the odds?

I'll never forget one experience, after having just finished my first movie... I was sitting in the edit room, cutting the movie together.

I was faced with an overwhelming feeling that the movie was coming to and end, and I'd be back to square one waiting for the world to come to me. It was a familiar feeling and anyone in the 'arts' will probably be somewhat familiar with it.

So out of this fear, I wrote my next movie, Foster. And guess what? Before we had finished editing my first film, I was on set with my next movie. My thoughts led to intention. My intention led to action. My actions led to opportunity. And that opportunity led to results.

You can be the greatest painter on earth. You could even have painted 300 works of art. But if they are all locked away in the loft of your house and you don't ever show them to the world, no one will ever know. If you don't go to the gallery and ask to have a show, you'll never know what could have been from the simple act of walking into the field to milk the cow.

And that's ok too, if that's what you want… but true inner happiness comes from a sense of earning things in your life, and most of us instinctively understand this.

THE BRIGHT IDEA

THE WORLD IS FULL OF LIGHT BULBS.

Every great entrepreneur or inventor has a light bulb moment. For the Wright brothers it was flight, for Edison it was literally the light bulb, and for me it was coconuts.

You may be reading this and not have had your light blub moment yet.

Or, you may have had your light bulb moment, tried to make the bulb, only to find there were already a dozen light bulbs already on the market.

You may have built your bulb only to run out of glass or filaments just after you made it.

You may have made your bulb only to realize that actually not many people actually want light bulbs, because people in this universe prefer candlelight. Light bulbs are expensive and only posh people with money buy light bulbs.

You may have built your light bulb, but painted it green, and made it square instead of circular, and people think it looks pretty ugly.

You might think that your light bulb is the greatest invention ever made, but no one else agrees with you.

In fact, there are so many permutations of things that can go wrong, that it's a wonder you ever made the light bulb in the first place!

My own light bulb moment came years after I first discovered coconuts. It was on that beach in Thailand that I fell in love with coconut water, but it wasn't until some years later , when I discovered it in a carton, read a bit about it and saw there was a big buzz about it in America, that the light bulb went off.

I am at a place now where I am always open to light bulb moments in my life.

I have light bulb moments all the time. Recently I thought how great it would be if high heel shoes had a detachable heel and the heels could convert to a flat! Or a hygienic potty that drains through a hole in the back rather than over the lip! These are light bulb moments borne out of everyday experiences (or mis-experiences). I also thought about a disposable bag of BBQ charcoal but shaped in a pyramid because a pyramid shape burns easier (by the way if any of you go and market any of these you know where to send commission to).

As the expression goes...

NECESSITY IS THE MOTHER OF INVENTION.

However, not all light bulb moments necessarily need further exploration or even invention. Sometimes simplicity is the better choice, as opposed to the over-engineered option to a problem where a problem does not exist in the first place.

Here is an illustration of a Victorian invention that never saw the light of day. It's a an umbrella that has spectacles built into the fabric!

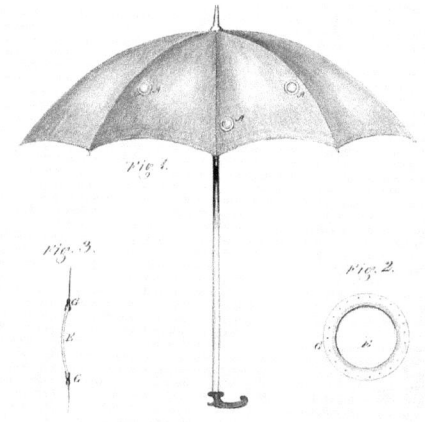

Here is a Japanese Mobile Toilet Paper Dispenser, which, for some reason, never took off:

Sometimes, all you need is just a pack of tissues tucked away into your pocket or bag.

Here is a Metro Chin Stick:

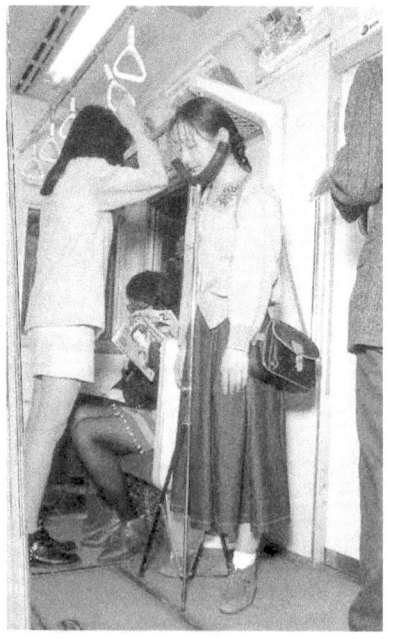

ROALD DAHL'S INCREDIBLE INVENTION

I have just written a screenplay about Roald Dahl. Both the story and the evolution of the story are quite relevant and truly fascinating.

I saw Matilda in the West End and as I sat there watching the show, it struck me that there had never been a biopic on Dahl, one of the most iconic authors the UK has ever produced. I duly bought all the biographies I could read. Whilst his life was fascinating, one of the books referenced a medical invention he had invented. This reference took up what amounted to one page in a five hundred page book.

In 1960, Dahl's 9 month old boy got hit by a taxi and suffered terrible brain damage. The doctors operated 9 times on this little boy, inserting a shunt into his brain to help drain the excess fluid (known as a hydrocephalus). 9 times, the shunt failed and had to be removed. Dahl was exasperated that medical science could not invent a valve that would not leak or not get blocked. He began reading medical books and learnt everything there was to know about hydrocephalus. He then got together was Stanley Wade, a toymaker who made engines in model airplanes. The engines had tiny parts, which were accurate to the thousandths of a millimeter. If Wade could build these parts, he argued, then he could help Dahl build a valve.

The two set upon a journey that culminated in a brand new patented medical shunt that ended up saving the lives of 3000 children! Whilst it has now been superseded, many people still have this shunt in their heads today.

Whilst the valve was Dahl's light bulb moment, bourn entirely out of necessity, the story that I read, that took up just one page of a 500 page biography, was my light bulb moment. When I told people about Dahl, I'd recount this incredible tail. So when it came time to write my story, I knew the story I wanted to tell...

GOLDEN RULES FOR A GREAT BUSINESS
1. HAS IT BEEN DONE BEFORE
2. INNOVATION
3. SCALABILITY

1. HAS IT BEEN DONE BEFORE

Let's face it, there are a finite number of ideas floating around in the world. Most likely, it's been done before.

The first thing you should do, after you've had your light bulb moment, is hit Google and see if anyone else has done it before.

If so, you need to answer these questions:

How late to the market are you?
Can you do something different than what is out there
Can you do something better than what is out there?

If you are quite late to the market it might be that the market is now saturated.

With my own coconut water business, I knew it was big in America already, and everything I read told me it was going to be big in the UK. But by the time I managed to raise the money for my company, there were already 5 or 6 brands on the market, making it a more competitive environment to launch my product.

I knew that whatever I did had to be better than what was already out there. It had to be better in terms of product, and better in terms of branding. It had to stand above the competition. That was my challenge.

Though I was late to the market, I didn't feel I was so late that I couldn't compete in the race. Would I launch a coconut water now? Absolutely not!

You have less chance of winning a marathon where there are 3000 people running and you are at the back.

If there are 5 people running and you are a few feet behind them, or at the same start point, odds are you can finish the race and you may actually win.

I was at a trade fair in Spain wondering around the enormous hall when I discovered freeze dried fruit. I wasn't looking for it. In fact, I met someone at my own stand who tried my coconut water and invited me round to their stand to try their products... freeze dried crisps.

I remember trying them and they were delicious. And I was so surprised at the unexpected crunch and lavor of freeze dried mango and crunchy broccoli crisps. It was a momentary revelation. I remember saying "these are amazing." And I also remember thinking that there was nothing like them in the UK and I think it could be very scalable. That was my light bulb moment.

ELON MUSK

Elon Musk, now the 39th richest person[3] in the world thanks to the invention of Paypal, (in itself pretty innovate) is using his wealth to create and invent some amazing things.

At the time of writing some of his more interesting ideas include:

the Tesla: a supercharged electric car
Mars X: a project to send greenhouses to Mars
The Hyperloop: a new superfast transportation system based on pressurized pods riding on an air cushion

UBER
Uber is another really great invention. Currently it has the UK taxi drivers completely up in arms as they've had a virtual monopoly on the UK taxi service until Uber came along.

Uber is an example of innovation in a scalable market with very little competition.

PRET A MANGER
Pret A Manger began life as one sandwich bar in Hampstead by Julian Metcalfe in 1984 and now turns over more than £600m per year. Now Julian runs ITSU and also Metcalfe's.

COFFEE REPUBLIC
Sahar & Bobby Hashemi formed Coffee Republic after coming back from New York and realized there was no place they could buy a decent cup of coffee. This was 1995 and well before the coffee shop revolution we know now.

GU
James Averdieck came up with the idea of luxury desserts while eating chocolate in Belgium. At the time there was a void in the supermarkets. The company was sold for £32m in 2010[4].

FACEBOOK
Mark Zuckerberg famously started facebook as a way to meet girls. Facebook now posts revenues of over $17 billion[5].

Whilst these are just small snapshots of some cool businesses, they were all created from nothing. One individual had an idea. They took that idea, turned it into intention and planted seeds which germinated.

I guarantee none of them were overnight sensations. They all took work and perseverance. All of these entrepreneurs 'earnt' their success – none of them were the result of charity or hand me downs.

---

4. http://www.thetimes.co.uk/tto/business/columnists/article3806353.ece
5. 10-K Annual Report". SEC Filings. Facebook. January 31, 2014. Retrieved February 7, 2014.

2. INNOVATION

How innovate is your product or idea?

This is the second question you must ask yourself before you embark on your business.

TYPES OF INNOVATION:
INNOVATION IN A TOTALLY NEW CATEGORY
INNOVATION IN AN EXISTING SPACE

If you are creating something completely new, which the market has NEVER seen before, that's pretty incredible, and hats off to you.

You now need to ask some objective questions:

IS THERE A NEED FOR THIS INNOVATION?
WILL ANYONE BUY IT?
WILL ANYONE WANT IT?
HOW NICHE IS IT?
HOW SCALABLE IS IT?
HOW EASY WILL IT BE TO GET TO MARKET?
WILL OTHERS FIND IT AS INTERESTING AS I DO OR AM I COMPLETELY SELF-DELUDED?!

If you are innovating in an existing space, you need to ask yourself these questions:

DOES IT DO SOMETHING DIFFERENT OR BETTER THAN WHAT ALREADY IS?
HOW COMPETITIVE AND CROWDED IS THIS MARKET PLACE? HOW LATE AM I TO MARKET?
WHAT SHARE OF THE MARKET DO YOU THINK YOU COULD GET INNOVATING IN THIS EXISTING SPACE?

I am constantly amazed at the new entrants to the coconut water category. The market is now quite well established yet every year I see new entrepreneurs launching brands. Most are just 'me too' brands, ie, nothing more than imitations of existing brands offering very little in the way of interesting branding let alone a unique product. Sadly, the majority of late entrants to the market do not survive past the first year of trading.

Occasionally I will see some innovation in the space, such as combining protein and coconut water. This was a good idea, because coconut water is used to hydrate, so making it accessible to the 'body building' market is a no brainer.

I love watching Dragon's Den to see some really balmy inventions. Generally it's clear to everyone but the person pitching just how insane and ridiculous some ideas are.

HERE'S JUST SOME OF THE TOP 10 CRAZIEST PITCHES THAT ENTERED THE DEN LOOKING FOR MONEY:

DRIVESAFE GLOVE
a single glove that you put on your right hand to remind you what side of the road to drive on

SHUC
a stick on device to hold shower heads when travelling to Greece

CARDBOARD BEACH FURNITURE
(self-explanatory!)

CUCUMBER CONDOM
plastic caps to stop the end of cucumbers going dry.

THROX
sox that come in 3s because one always goes missing!

PET BURIAL PACK
A Cone to put on top of your dog poo

BACON SCENTED ALARM CLOCK

CAFFEINE LACED WAFFLES

THE URO CLUB
designed for golfers who need to pee – a hollow golf club that allows you to stick it in and let it out. This one really takes the piss.

3. SCALABILITY

The final question you need to ask yourself is how scalable you think your idea can be. In other words, how big could you potentially get.

SCALABILITY GIVES YOU A MEASURE OF HOW BIG YOUR PRODUCT IS VS HOW BIG THE MARKET IS. WHAT IS THE SIZE OF THE PRIZE?

There is nothing intrinsically wrong with small, niche products. In fact they are great, provide a fabulous service and often have the most integrity.

Some of my favorite products in the food world are small and niche. Just walk into Whole Foods or Planet Organic and you'll see some amazing and beautiful brands: from delicious artisan chocolates, to raw granolas, to cold-pressed juices. These may never be 'mass market' products, but sometimes integrity of product is more interesting, or more important, than money. They really provide a fantastic service, even if they will never be hugely commercial.

NICHE BREAKOUTS

Sometimes, your love and passion for your niche product engages the masses and becomes commercial, like coconut water has done. There are also some other niche products in the drinks category, such as Birch Water, Maple Water, Artichoke Water all trying to achieve the same breakout success that coconut water has had.

In the food world, Sushi is a really great example of a breakout success. You wouldn't think it now, but the thought of eating raw fish in the 1990s was solely a Japanese owned cultural phenomenon or for those shipwrecked on a dingy in the middle of the Pacific.

I remember my friend Doug, who was studying Japanese, took me to my first sushi restaurant in 1992 whilst I was in college in Boston. It was not trendy, nor was it very common back then. I can't think of any other niche food that has had the same incredible breakout success as sushi as had.

Let's face it, no one else, apart from the British, have embraced Marmite in quite the same way.

You see niche breakouts in every industry. Think about toy fads, clothing fads, and technological fads. Some of them are just fads and don't last, others are more enduring.

Often, if your pockets are deep enough, you can drive innovation. No one does this better than APPLE.

Apple really revolutionized our lives – from the way we listen to music, to the way smartphones have been integrated into our lives.

As we know from Newton's 3rd law, for every action there is an equal and opposite reaction. Apple's innovations have both improved our lives, but also made them worse. We now interact more with our telephone than with each other. Social interactions have changed in the space of 20 years. Our interactions with our friends have become more virtual than physical, and we share more experiences with our friends through the click of a button. This is the sad trade off for technological innovation.

The answer to scalability is really based on how big you want to be. Being scalable means your product has potential. It also means you can move it from your garage to more industrial sized manufacturing.

You may be making cashew butter in your garage, but what happens when cashew butter becomes the rage? How will you scale this up? And can you scale this up? And do you have the money and enough cashews to scale up?

If you really want to build a successful business you need to remember and understand my three golden rules:

> **HAS IT BEEN DONE BEFORE**
> **INNOVATION**
> **SCALABILITY**

GOODS VS SERVICES

I recently had an epiphany about my own business. It seems rather an obvious one to me when I think about it, but it's worth sharing with you. It hit me after staring at my own Profit and Loss Sheet for too long!

THERE ARE TWO TYPES OF BUSINESSES:
SELLING GOODS OR SELLING SERVICES

If you are in the business of selling goods, you are buying or making a widget from somewhere and then selling it. The widget costs, say £50 and you sell it for, let's say, £100. That gives you a £50 gross profit, or a 50% gross profit margin.

If you are in the business of selling services, you are selling time or labour. For example, let's say you are a graphic designer and someone commissions you to create a logo. If you sell that logo for £100, there were no direct expenses involved, and so you have £100 gross profit.

Your time, wages, etc, all come out of your operating expenses (as they would in the first example of selling goods).

You have no cost of goods or direct expenses in the actual creation of that logo as you would in the initial scenario of selling goods.

If you want to make good margins, the moral here is to start a service related business. That's why so many dotcom businesses, internet sites, and apps have been able to monetize so well.

BRANDBUILDING
WHAT IS YOUR BRAND?

Apart from the quality of your product, your brand identity is the single most important element of your product.

Using food or drink as an example, think about the last time you went into a supermarket and browsed the shelf.

95% of purchasing decisions happen on impulse in front of the shelf. And it all happens in a flash. Your eyes scan the shelves and process information like a superfast computer, making choices on what looks nice and what is the right price. You are collecting and compiling data in milliseconds.

Your could have the most amazing product on the planet, but if it's misbranded, it can fail.

So don't underestimate the importance of this process. At the beginning of your journey, it's the one area where it's important to spend money. Otherwise it's a false economy. Imagine getting that product to market having hired a second rate designer on the cheap, only to realize 1 year in your product is not selling and it's all down to the branding. It's better to spend the time and money on the beginning getting it right.

There are three areas you need to consider.

NAME

LOGO

IMAGE

NAME

What's in a name? Almost everything.

Think of some iconic brands: Innocent, GU, Coke, The White Company, KFC, Apple.

Here's a few more with their logos:

First, a word of warning... remember to Google your brand name and check no one else has used it! Also check the trademark registers in your country, and also top level domains (.com). Don't go down the route of launching something that exists somewhere already. It's too risky and ultimately will have legal repercussions down the line. Rebranding product is expensive, not to mention all the customers you will lose who may have gotten used to your brand name.

YOU HAVE TWO TYPES OF NAMES:

THE ONES THAT HIT THE NOSE, AND THE OTHER THAT CAPTURES THE ESSENCE.

WHICH IS MORE INTERESTING?

Initially the name for my brand was YOCOCO. I think you'd agree this hits the nose because it has 'coco' in the actual brand name. The best thing I ever could have done was to explore more brand names. CHI means life force, and I think you'll agree captures the essence of my brand.

And looking back now at the other brands on the market, the majority of them have the word 'coco' in the title: Vita Coco, Cocofina, Go Coco, Coco Pro, Coco Libre, Cocotien, Coco Za, Zico, Jax Coco, Coco Quench. And that's just a small selection! Do you want to be a 'me too' brand – just a carbon copy of everything out there? Strive for originality and don't settle until you get it.

Imagine if the brand name for GU was actually "ChocoPuds"? GU is suggestive of oozing chocolate, and it also suggests something foreign. It's short and sweet and to the point and you can also launch anything under it, not just chocolate puds.

Imagine if "Innocent" was "The Juice Smoothie Company". The name Innocent suggests purity, lack of preservatives or chemicals, and 'just the fruit'.

Sometimes you *want* brands to be on the nose, like Kentucky Fried Chicken – because it does what it says on the tin. And you will generally find that generic brands, or supermarket brands will go down the safe route in terms of name and packaging. There is nothing inherently wrong with that... it's just not very interesting. And to be interesting is more interesting than being safe.

REGISTERING YOUR TRADEMARK

Now that you have a name you should really register your trademark, at the very least, in the country you are trading in. A lawyer can assist you with this (though they will charge you much more than the actual cost of registering it), or, if you are not afraid of form filling, you can do this yourself too and save some money. I'd also recommend filing a European Community Trademark which gives you protection across the EU.

Here are some links to get started:

UK TRADEMARKS, INTELLECTUAL PROPERTY OFFICE:
https://www.gov.uk/topic/intellectual-property/trade-marks

EUROPEAN COMMUNITY TRADEMARK:
https://oami.europa.eu/ohimportal/en/

USA TRADEMARK & PATENTS OFFICE:
http://www.uspto.gov/

TAKING RISKS

Why play it safe?

It's like choosing an outfit. You can go for the plain black number, or you be a little more daring, a little more adventurous and pick a colour. Black has been done before... many times...! Be original and be bold and don't be afraid to step out of your comfort zone. The same is to be said of packaging design.

Here is a picture of our coconut Milk:

When you think of milk, you think of a white carton, right? The obvious route for this product was a white carton. The decision to go black felt risky to us.

But then I asked myself the question "what is more interesting?" A white carton or a black one... I kept coming back to the idea of going against the grain.

Here is a copy of the white packaging. Granted it looks nice – but then, everything else we do is white, and we also needed to differentiate our coconut milks from our 'coconut waters'.

You will obviously form your own opinion, and it may be different to mine, but at the end of the day, you only have you instinct to rely on.

Time will tell if we made the right choice!

WHAT IS YOUR PRODUCT?

Define what it is and whom it's for. You need to know both your market and your demographic. Understanding these key elements helps you design your brand.

It can help if you put together a mood board, which is both reflective of wording and imagery.

On the next few pages, take a look at the following three mood boards I made for CHI.

You can see that each are positioned in a different demographic:

WELL BEING REVIVER
Lifestyle

ELIXIR OF LIFE
Yoga

NATURAL HYDRATION
Sports

I used these boards to show focus groups at the time because we weren't sure what was the strongest concept and what would hit the highest demographic.

Elixir of Life

Take time out from your busy day to escape to our Yococo spa on the shores of Thailand, fringed with swaying palms. Pour yourself an ice cold Yococo and taste the invigorating elixir of life that only 100% pure coconut water can deliver. This purely natural water drink tastes delicious and comes straight from young coconuts and is bottled at source in Thailand. It's packed full of goodness and will leave you feeling so Zen that you will not want to come back. Escape again, enjoy Yococo.

Natural Well-Being Reviver

It is important to drink plenty of water in our daily lives, to keep us healthy and vibrant. Now we would like to introduce you to Yococo, the fresh coconut water drink, which is better for us than water itself. Yococo is 100% unique, it has naturally energizing ingredients, such as sugars and electrolytes that will keep your body balanced and healthy. It's fat free, low in calories, and organic. So for the ultimate well-being drinking pleasure, try Yococo.

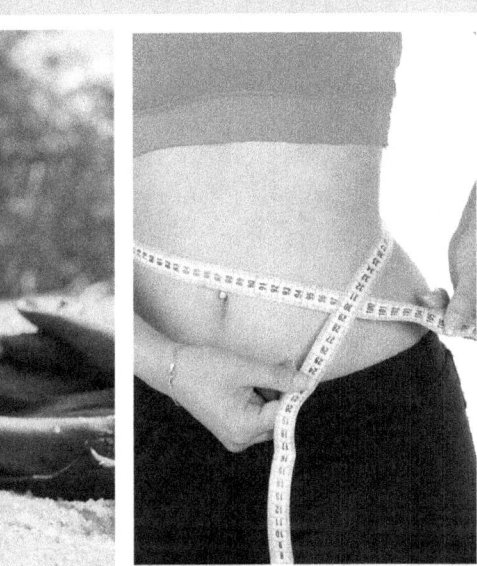

Pure Rehydration

When we finish a vigorous workout, the first thing we do is reach for an isotonic drink, to quench our thirst and replenish the goodness that we have lost. Yococo have harnessed nature to bring you 100% pure coconut water straight from the fruit, the completely natural hydrator. Full of natural goodness with a balance of five essential electrolytes. Yococo has naturally occurring sugars and salts, which are absorbed into the bloodstream four times quicker than water. Yococo is also more efficient to absorb than many sports drinks. It's fat free, organic and low in calories, so there's all the instant goodness you need, straight from nature.

This is where market research can come in handy. You may not be able to commission a market research firm to run a report for you, but there are plenty of ways of researching the market yourself – from surveying friends, strangers or running a focus group. None of these have to really cost anything.

Again, remember there is no one definitive answer. Whilst you might get a lot of people saying the same thing, you must trust your instinct when it comes to making decisions about the direction to go, and sometimes that has to be going against popular opinion. The loudest voice in the room can sometimes sway groups, so it's important to survey enough people.

PACKAGING HIERARCHY

Hierarchy means what you put on the pack and in what order.

Great branding should tell you:
WHAT IT IS
WHO IT IS
WHAT IT DOES
WHERE IT'S FROM

AND IT NEEDS TO TELL YOU ALL THAT....
IN ONE SECOND

The above designs were my original designs for CHI. Apart from the design itself you can see we looked at 3 types of structural packaging.

I had this designed originally for $350 by a freelancer, by the way. There are a number of flaws with the design. For me, the biggest flaws are in the hierarchy of the messages. Whenever you put 'what the product is' on the base of the pack, the eye has to work twice as hard at identifying it. The Logo takes up far too much of the pack and dominates the other elements. The other danger is that the 'what it is' gets lost when on a shelf, and if it's in shelf ready packaging (ie, a box) you won't see it at all.

The following few pages show the evolution of CHI and how I got to the final design:

OR LESS!

WHAT NOT TO DO:

This image (or a copy of it) is currently being used on dozens of brands. That's a big no-no!

CHI PRELIMINARY LOGO DESIGNS

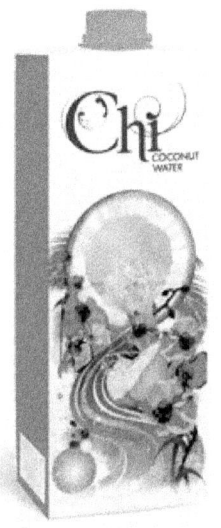

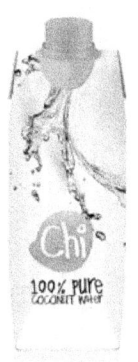

CHI FINAL DESIGN

WHAT IT IS

WHO IT IS

WHAT IT DOES

WHERE IT'S FROM

There are obviously some really lovely ideas our agency came up with in the development stage, and we could have gone in a number of different directions.

What I like about our current design is the ease and speed with which your eye gets the information it needs. It says what it is, who it is, what it does and where it's from... in a split second.

We had the image especially commissioned and you'll see it is symmetrical and a mirror image from side to side. It gives you a subconscious feel of balance, hydration (the waterfall), provenance, (ie, where it's from - which is our own special CHI island complete with lotus flowers, birds of paradaise plants, birds and is suggestive of Thailand).

What I most like is that there is NO coconut at all on the front.

FINAL THOUGHTS

If you are on a budget, there are plenty of freelancers who will do a cracking design for you.

HERE ARE A COUPLE WEBSITES WHERE YOU CAN ADVERTISE YOUR JOBS:

https://www.upwork.com

https://www.blurgroup.com/

PART 2

HOW TO RUN AND SUSTAIN A BUSINESS
(AND MAKE MONEY ALONG THE WAY)

FORMING A COMPANY

You have several choices when starting out and there are different tax implications for each one.

It is a good idea, at this stage, to speak with your accountant who can advise you on the best choice for you. The most common is a Limited Company.

HERE ARE THE MAIN ONES:

LIMITED COMPANY

Forming a limited company is often a very good idea. Your liability is 'limited', meaning that if you do encounter problems, you are not personally responsible for debt. Each member will have shares and you will need to file accounts as well as form articles of association, memorandum and a shareholding agreement.

SOLE TRADER

A sole trader is run by one person. Hence there is no distinction between company and individual. That means you have unlimited liability for all debts! Be careful!

LLP

A Limited Liability Partnership is one where several partners form a company, but where the liabilities are limited to that partner. In other words, you are not responsible for your partner's negligence or misconduct should something go awry.

PLC

A Public Limited Company is one where the shares are traded on a public platform (ie a stock exchange). There are strict rules governing forming a PLC and very costly to setup. It's therefore generally not an option for start-ups.

CIO

A Charitable Incorporated Organisation is designed for non-profit organisations.

The most common (and sensible) option is to form a limited company. It will ultimately protect you personally should the company go under.

COMPANIES HOUSE

To register your company you need to do this through Companies House:
https://www.gov.uk/government/organisations/companies-house

Your accountant can also register it for you. Remember to do a search first to check that your company name has not been taken.

Also remember that having a ltd company also means filing documents such as accounts and annual returns. Your company can also be dormant, and you should speak to your accountant about this if you wish to register the company name but do not plan to trade for a while. Registering your company name *is not* the same as registering a trademark. So just because you have the company name with companies house does not give you automatic protection for copyright or trademark infringement.

Also, if you wish to open a bank account in your ltd company name, you will need to have registered your company already with companies house, as banks will not let you until you have completed this step.

FORMING A BUSINESS PLAN

If you are serious about raising money you'll need to have a business plan. I'm including a sample plan in the appendix.

Here are the sections you should consider including in your plan:

COVER PAGE
Make it visual throughout. Everyone likes pictures!

EXECUTIVE SUMMARY
What is your business about, what does it do, what problem does it solve, why is it unique

COMPANY OVERIEW
Where you are based, details of your company infrastructure, perhaps what success your company has already achieved.

INDUSTRY ANALYSIS
An overview of the market, include stats

CUSTOMER ANAYLYSIS:
An overiew of your demographic and customer base.

COMPETITIVE ANALYSIS:
An overview of your competition – include their strengths and Weakneseses – try aslo including a SWOT analysis (more following)

MARKETING PLAN:
Include your plan for marketing. If you can divide into Below the Line (promotions etc) and above the line (TV, Print, radio)

OPERATIONS PLAN:
How will you be run day to day and who and what do you need to make this happen.

MANAGEMENT TEAM

Who will run it and what are their past accomplishments. You may want to mention any gaps in your teams and future hires.

FINANCIAL PLAN

Critical to investors. How will you make money, Cash Flow Forecasts for 3 years (a Summary and in full in your appendix). What the funds will be used for.

APPENDIX

Anything else useful that you need to add

Be creative, be visual, and also be realistic. Don't be tempted to overegg your financials so much that they appear arbitrary. Savvy investors can see through high numbers. You could always do a best case/worse scenario.

EIS QUALIFYING

EIS
Enterpise Investment Scheme.

This is a tax scheme that the government introduced to make investment in UK qualifying companies attractive to investors. It basically works by offering the investor tax relief up to 30% of the cost of the shares up to a maximum of £1,000,000 investment (so the investor can claim a tax deduction on £300,000 for example). Generally the shares have to be held for 3 years in order to qualify for relief.

This is an excellent scheme and it is worth ensuring you qualify for EIS by checking with your accountant.

MORE INFO:

https://www.gov.uk/government/publications/the-enterprise-investment-scheme-introduction/enterprise-investment-scheme

SAMPLE SWOT ANALYSIS

A SWOT analysis is an objective way to view your company or business. Often we just glorify the positive without considering the negative. A SWOT shows that you understand the potential threats and weaknesses of your business.

S = STRENGTHS

W = WEAKNESSES

O = OPPORTUNITIES

T = THREATS

Below is a SWOT I made for CHI when I first launched. I made this for free online through a program called GLIFFY.

https://www.gliffy.com/uses/swot-analysis-software/

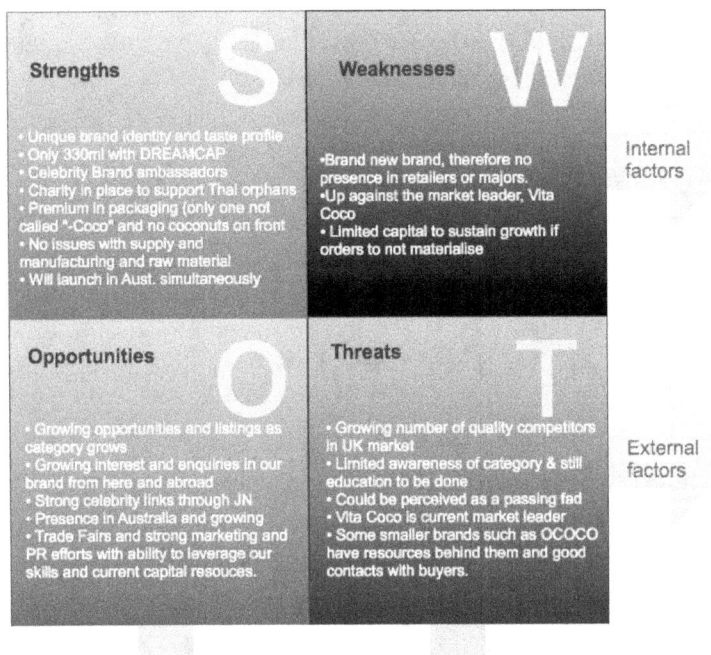

MONEY

"In 2012, according to Bis.gov, more than 400,000 new businesses were set up. However 20% of those new businesses failed within the first year and 50 per cent won't be around by 2015."[6]

I think it's fair to say that many businesses fail within the first year. This can be down to a number of factors: poor product, bad execution, lack of sales, etc.

HOWEVER, THE SINGLE BIGGEST PROBLEM OF WHY BUSINESSES FAIL IS OFTEN CASH FLOW.

When I was launching CHI, a distributor told me I needed a minimum of £500k to launch a brand. I launched mine on £200k and even that was tough! No matter how much you have in the bank, it goes quicker than it comes. All you need is one 'bad debt' (a bad debt is when someone does not pay an invoice), and you can suddenly find yourself in serious trouble. More on bad debts later in the section on credit insurance.

WHY YOU NEED IT

Most companies start life underfunded.

Your chances of surviving in this arena are drastically reduced if you launch with no money. I've seen many companies run by friends who have gone bankrupt because they never had enough money to start with. They were constantly chasing their tail, skirting above zero, until finally their expenses just far outweighed their income and they closed shop. It's very sad to see entrepreneurs who have poured their heart and soul, blood, sweat and tears into something, only for it to implode. Don't let this be you.

By the way, the reason I wrote the first half of this book is because you need to embrace the mindset of failure in order to sail through the rocky waters that lay ahead... like not having enough money. So if you skipped it, please go back now and read it!

No matter what your business is, your initial start-up costs can be large, not even including your monthly overheads. If you are in manufacturing, it is quite likely your supplier will have MOQs (minimum order requirements). And in order to always have stock, you'll always need to be purchasing in quantities that far exceed your rate of sale (ROS).

HOW TO GET MONEY

Broadly speaking, money for your business can be divided into two categories: *Debt and Equity.*

Debt is money that is loaned to the company. This could be in the form of the bank loan, a director's loan or anyone else that *loans* the company money. Debt remains on your books and is eventually repayable. Debt from a bank is often secured against assets (things you own), so they might ask you to pledge your house in exchange. Many banks will lend unsecured loans up to £25k (and so will some credit card companies) so this could be something to look into.

Equity is money that is given to the company in exchange for shareholding. It can be from friends, family, private equity firms, venture capital firms. Equity is generally not repayable and investors' money is at risk should the company go bankrupt.

WHERE TO LOOK FOR DEBT

BANKS, BUILDING SOCIETIES, CREDIT UNIONS:
It is a good idea to speak to your bank and also other high street banks and see what you may be able to borrow. Various options are available in the form of a loan, an overdraft facility, a credit line, invoicing factoring, equipment leasing and asset financing.

CROWD-FUNDING:
There are some interesting crowd based lending platforms. Try Funding Circle to get started.
https://www.fundingcircle.com

EFG LOAN:
At the time of writing there is also a very interesting Government backed scheme called the *Enterprise Finance Guarantee Scheme (EFG)*. This is a loan by a bank but the government will guarantee 75% of the loan. There are some hoops to jump through but it's worth it. I have borrowed £300,000 from the banks through an EFG loan and highly recommend it. Hopefully the scheme will stay in place.

For more info:
https://www.gov.uk/guidance/understanding-the-enterprise-finance-guarantee

SUPPLIER CREDIT:
This can be a powerful tool in managing your cash flow. Suppliers offer credit for payment of goods. Try to negotiate longer terms for payments, ie 60 days.

FACTORING COMPANIES:
Many companies will lend money against the value of invoices you may have on your books from customers. Banks do this too but they generally will insist on managing your entire ledger (ie, they will lend money on ALL the invoices owed to you and ask for a separate bank account for your customers to pay into). There are also some factoring companies that will lend on just

one invoice, such as Market Invoice (I've personally used it and it's great).

htttps://www.marketinvoice.com

htttps://www.investly.co

WHERE TO LOOK FOR EQUITY

FRIENDS & FAMILY:
Don't be afraid to ask your existing network of friends and family. If you don't ask you don't get! And if they can't help, ask them if they know anyone. Quite often, money comes from close to home.

PRIVATE EQUITY/VENTURE CAPITAL:
There are a gazillion firms that will give money in exchange for shareholding. A quick GOOGLE for "Private Equity" will bring them up. Don't contact them until you have a business plan. Also many won't look at start-ups, so it's not always the best place to start. It's generally better when you have 2-3 years of trading accounts behind you.

FAMILY OFFICES:
Surprisingly, few people know about family offices. They manage the money of wealthy families. This can be a very interesting and underused route for accessing finance. It takes some research, but cast the net wide and you may catch a fish.

CROWD-FUNDING:
If you haven't heard about crowd funding you've had your head buried in the sand. To sum it up, you post details of your project on a web platform, the amount you are looking to raise and offer perks to people who invest in the form of shares of other things.

HERE ARE A FEW TO GET YOU STARTED:

CROWD-CUBE: htttps://www.crowdcube.com
INDIEGOGO: htttps://www.indiegogo.com
GROW THE DECK: htttps://www.growthdeck.com

JUST GIVING: https://crowdfunding.justgiving.com
CROWDFUNDER: http://www.crowdfunder.co.uk/
SEEDRS/KICKSTARTER: https://wwwlseedrs.com/
SYNDICATE ROOM: https://www.syndicateroom.com/
INVESTING ZONE: https://www.syndicateroom.com/

I was told by an insider that generally crowdfunding works best when you start the campaign with 100% already committed. That's because campaigns that start off with zero money, don't look very attractive to potential investors and have less success of closing.

REMEMBER, MONEY ATTRACTS MONEY!

ANGEL'S DENS

You may have watched Dragon's Den before, but there are also many real life clubs around the country where wealthy investors go to look for the next big thing.

These can be hit and miss and I advise you to research these well. Some will ask for up front money and so you must weigh up the risk of forking up some dough and the likelihood of getting investment. Most will work on a success fee of funds invested. There are some good clubs out there so do your homework. And beware of false prophets!

THE INNER CIRCLE:
http://innercircleclub.co.uk/

This was set up by Patricia and Ken Anderson. Apart from being a networking club to be a part of, it's also a place where entrepreneurs can pitch their businesses over dinner to high net worth individuals, family offices, and private equity firms. There is a fee for dinner (and joining the club if you wish to), and they regularly hold dinners every fortnight.

GOVERNMENT GRANTS & SCHEMES

If you do your research there are also a number of grants available and government back schemes.

HERE ARE A FEW TO GET YOU STARTED:

NESTA:
http://www.nesta.org.uk/get-funding

GOV.UK:
https://www.gov.uk/business-finance-support-finder/search

GOVERNMENT FUNDING:
http://governmentfunding.org.uk/

MANUFACTURING ADVISE SERVICE (MAS)
http://www.mas.bis.gov.uk/

UK TRADE & INVESTMENT:
https://www.gov.uk/government/organisations/uk-trade-investment

REGIONAL GROWTH FUND:
https://www.gov.uk/government/organisations/uk-trade-investment

BUSINESS ACCELERATORS

This is a fairly newish concept. These companies help small businesses get investment ready and take equity in exchange. If you don't feel you can do it yourself they can be a good place to start. However if you can do it yourself, you are needlessly giving away valuable equity.

The following page has a comprehensive list of UK based accelerators:

http://entrepreneurhandbook.co.uk/business-accelerators/

MANAGING MONEY

Now that you've (hopefully!) raised money for your business, formed your company and opened your bank account, your next job is to not run out of it. We'll talk about cash flow in the next chapter and how to best manage cash.

Managing money can be the single most challenging aspect of running a business.

BOOK-KEEPING

Typically, most small business owners are somewhat 'scared' of doing their own book-keeping. However, gone are the days of needing to hire a book-keeper. The world has evolved and so has technology.

There are a number of software programs on the market however I am only going to recommend one, because in my opinion, it's the best on the market and the easiest to use!

IT'S CALLED XERO:
https://www.xero.com/

XERO

Xero is a cloud based accounting and book-keeping system. It costs about £10-£25 per month depending on your needs. Trust me, it is WELL worth every penny if not more. For the record, I'm not on commission... but I recommend this program to everyone I meet because not only is it easy to use, teaches you everything you need to know about book-keeping and finance, but it's fun (if accounting can be fun!) and makes it a pleasure to use day to day. If you are ysing anything else, please ditch it and move to Xero. You can even import from your current software program like Sage. Also, it is best and easiest to start using it at the beginning of your financial year if you are making the switch.

HERE ARE JUST SOME OF THE FEATURES OF XERO:

CASHFLOW
- ONLINE ACCOUNTING
- INVENTORY
- AUTOMATIC BANK RECONCILIATION
- SMART REAL TIME REPORTS
- FILE STORAGE
- MULTI-CURRENCY ACCOUNTING

INVOICING
- EASY INVOICING
- SEND INVOICE REMINDERS
- SEND QUOTES
- CREDIT NOTES

PAYMENTS
- CLAIM EXPENSES
- ENTER BILLS
- CREATE PURCHASE ORDERS
- CREDIT NOTES

REPORTS
- FINANCIAL REPORTING ON EVERYTHING
- FIXED ASSETS

PAYROLL
- PAY YOUR EMPLOYEES

SUBMISSIONS
- SUBMIT VAT RETURNS TO HMRC
- PRINT OUT EU SALES REPORTS

CONTACTS
- ORGANISE CUSTOMERS AND SUPPLIERS
- CREATE SMART LISTS

MOBILE
- GO MOBILE!

It does so much more though! I strongly urge you to get stuck in and use xero every day yourself. I promise it's easy to learn as the interface is very user friendly.

HERE ARE JUST SOME OF THE THINGS I PERSONALLY LOVE ABOUT XERO:

IT PULLS IN YOUR BANK TRANSACTIONS AND YOU CAN EASILY FILE THEM IN THE CORRECT 'CHART OF ACCOUNTS.'

YOU CAN CREATE INVOICES AND SEND THEM TO CLIENTS.

IT'S COMPLETELY PAPERLESS SO YOU CAN DRAG AND DROP BILLS OR PURCHASE ORDERS DIRECTLY ONTO THE SCREEN AND IT ATTACHES TO THE CORRECT PAGE.

YOU CAN SEE WHO OWES YOU MONEY EASILY, AND SET UP REMINDERS TO BE SENT TO CUSTOMERS.

YOU CAN ALSO SEE WHAT MONEY YOU OWE AT A GLANCE.

YOU CAN PRINT OUT A MANAGEMENT REPORT, A PROFIT AND LOSS SHEET, A BALANCE SHEET AND YOU CAN ALSO FORECAST.

IT ALSO COMPLETELY INTEGRATES WITH SOME HMRC FUNCTIONS. FOR EXAMPLE, YOU CAN FILE YOUR VAT RETURN DIRECTLY FROM XERO WITHOUT HAVING TO ENTER THE HMRC PORTAL.

IF YOU SELL OVERSEAS YOU CAN ALSO PRINT OUT AN EU SALES REPORT WHICH YOU ARE OBLIGATED TO FILE WITH HMRC.

XERO
SCREENSHOTS

Using XERO will train you, without you knowing it, into the basics of accounting. I guarantee, if you use this on a daily basis, that after a few months you'll be a pro and it will completely transform the way you run your business.

I could write a whole chapter on how to use Xero, but just login for the free trial and have a play. They have an extensive help section and video tutorials.

Finally, at the end of your financial year, all you need to do is give your accountant access to Xero, and they'll be able to login and print out their own reports for submission to HMRC.

Amazing for a little accounts program that started life in New Zealand in 2006!
You can sign up for a 30 day trial online and also there are often promotional deals going on, so be sure to check here:
http://www.xero.com/uk/pricing

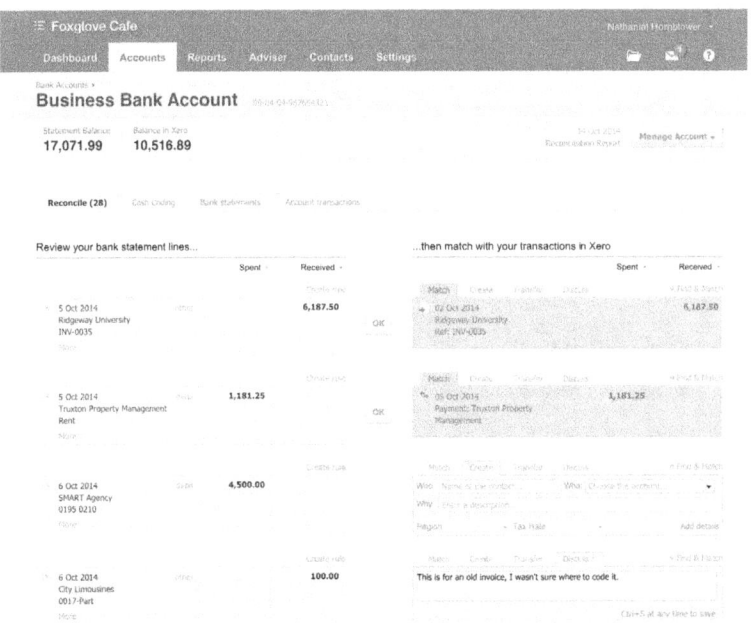

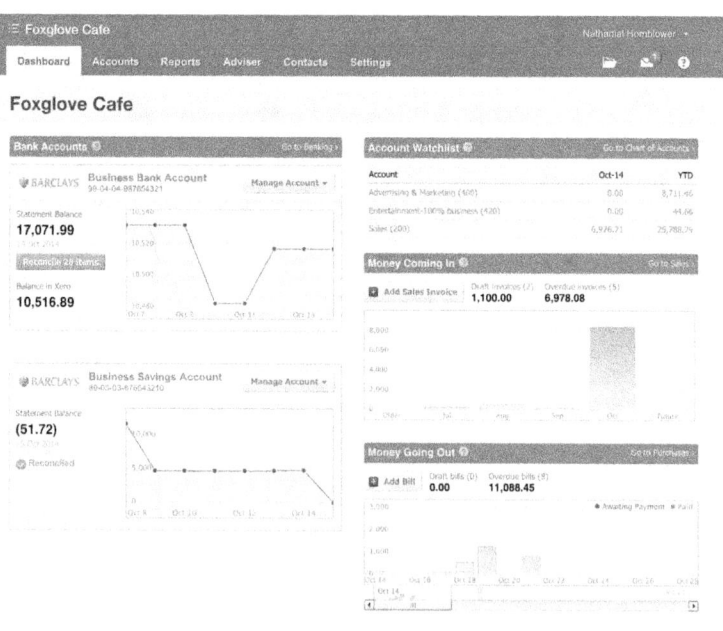

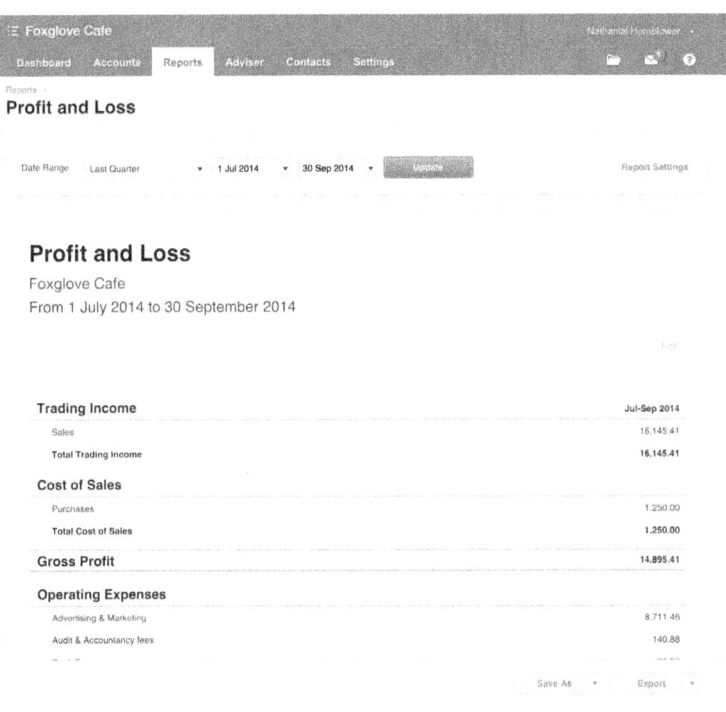

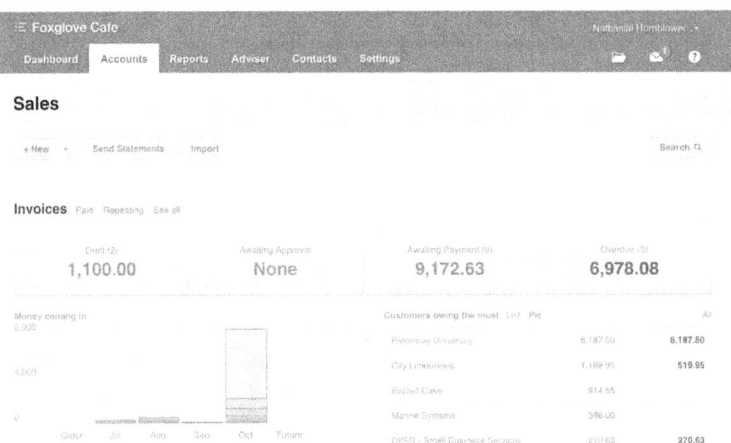

CASH FLOW

WHAT IS IT?

Typically, you will be chasing customers for payment of invoices while simultaneously attempting to pay your own bills.

CASH FLOW CAN BE DEFINED AS:
MONEY THAT FLOWS IN WHILE AT THE SAME TIME GOING OUT.

Cash flow is the death of many businesses, small and large. I will teach you some very basic tricks to help you manage your cash flow. If you get these in place from the start, your business has a far greater chance of longevity.

WHY IT'S IMPORTANT

Your business should be set up in such a way that it is able to self-fund the business cycle. Of course, there may be times in all business's lives where you need to do a fund raise.

However, you want to try to set up your business in such a way that cash does not go out faster than it comes in.

In my own business, I typically have to order full container loads of stock from my suppliers in Thailand. The value of each container can typically cost me £60,000. I need quite a few of these every month. However I don't sell £60,000 worth of stock in one go, because I have many customers that order at different times and have different payment terms. Therefore the challenge for me is how to finance the stock purchases when I haven't sold all the stock. This is a fairly typical scenario in any business that buys and sells goods. The bigger you get and the more you expand, the harder it becomes. That's because, as there is more demand for your product, you have to stomp up more cash to ensure you constantly have stock and do not go 'short'.

If you are a start-up, I highly advise ordering less stock than you need right now. You don't want to be sitting on stock that does not have a home... even worse if that stock has a shelf life and is perishable (like food). It may cost you more to make, but it may be a better call, at least in the beginning, so that you are not sitting on stock you have to throw away (of which the value will be much higher). So your margins, to start with, may not be as high, but you can work towards better margins when your volumes pick up.

YOU SHOULD ALWAYS NEGOTIATE LOWER PRICES BASED ON HIGHER VOLUMES WITH YOUR SUPPLIER.

HOW CASH FLOW CAN DESTROY YOU.

If you are not careful, you will find that your invoices quickly pile up, so that your expenses far outweigh the value of your invoices. This is a dangerous scenario to be in. Xero can be a godsend for this, as it shows you, in real time, what's coming in and what's going out. So if you are using the software everyday, you should be able to see, well in advance, if you are going to have a problem.

PRACTICAL SOLUTIONS FOR KEEPING YOUR BUSINESS RUNNING AND NOT RUNNING OUT OF MONEY

Ok, so how do you master cash flow? How do you reduce what goes out and maximize what goes in?

MONEY OUT = EXPENSES
negotiate long payment terms

MONEY IN = INVOICES
negotiate short payment terms

Here are a few tips and tricks that you need to get in place from day one.

CREDIT TERMS WITH YOUR SUPPLIERS

CREDIT TERM can be defined as the length of time which you are given to pay your bills, of the length of time you give a customer to pay his or her bill.

The trick, here, is to put off paying for your goods for as long as you can. How long?

AS LONG AS YOU POSSIBLY CAN!

This will be a negotiation. As a starting point, ask for 60 days. If they say no, ask for 45. It might be that you are a new customer and they will ask for pro-forma payment (ie, payment up front). If this is the case, get creative – ask for 50% on order and the balance on 30 days after delivery of goods. As you can see there are many permutations. If you have to stump up the cash up front in the beginning, wait until you have built up some trust with the supplier and go back and ask for credit terms again. This is one of the single most important negotiations you can make that will effect how your business is run and determine how much money you have in the bank at any given time.

Always pay your suppliers on time, if not early. If you build up a level of trust they will be more likely to support you in times of difficulty. If you do have trouble paying a bill (to anyone), don't dodge your supplier. Call them up before hand and explain things might be tight, and why, and commit to paying on a certain date. Suppliers prefer this honest approach and it is better than silence. And then be sure to actually stick to your word and pay when you said you would.

CREATIVE PAYMENT TERMS

When I first started supplying Pret A Manger in the UK, I realized cash flowing the stock I needed to ensure I could supply them would be difficult. One thing was certain... I did not want to run out of stock. The other thing I knew was that buying my stock from Asia, it was extremely difficult to get any form of credit terms. Most Thai factories require pro-forma payment, or at least payment by the time the goods arrive or they will refuse to release the BOL (Bill of Lading, which is a shipping document).

THIS IS WHEN I GOT CREATIVE.

I found a third party, in this case, a UK based ingredient supplier. I met with them and asked if they'd be willing to purchase for me from my supplier but extend some decent credit terms to me. We worked out a one-page deal memo, whereby they were not allowed to purchase coconut water or resell the water they were buying for me to anyone else. What they would receive was a small margin (1%) and a small finance fee (.5%). In return, they paid for the goods in advance, shipped the goods by freight, paid for the duty and tax and delivered the raw material to my warehouse in Germany at the time. Then, when I called in the raw material to be packed, I would have 60 days to pay for the raw material.

Suddenly, instead of having to spend £60k in advance, I had stock stored in the EU, and a further 60 days to pay for it only after I asked for it. This completely transformed the landscape of my business and was the single most important element that was instrumental in my growth.

I VALUED THIS RELATIONSHIP SO MUCH THAT I ALWAYS PAID ON TIME AND SOMETIMES EARLY.

When it came time to expand, I asked if they could finance 14 containers for me in advance. The trust had been created and they helped out again.

And only recently I had a bit of a traffic jam of invoices. Foreseeing this, I called up and explained the situation, why it was happening and when they would receive payment. Of course they were gracious in allowing me to pay late, knowing that I had the integrity to stick to my word (and if you read the first half of this book, now you know why integrity is so important).

LETTERS OF CREDIT (LOC)

This is another creative way to pay your suppliers and is generally offered by your bank. This is essentially a letter from your bank guaranteeing to your supplier that you will pay on time, and if you don't, the bank will cover the payment. If you deal with Asia this IS something they will accept.

INVOICING

THE SECOND MOST CRUCIAL PART OF THE CASH FLOW EQUATION IS INVOICING.

THE PAYMENT TERMS YOU OFFER YOUR CUSTOMERS, NOW THAT YOU ARE ON THE OTHER SIDE OF THE COIN, SHOULD BE AS SHORT AS POSSIBLE, AND, EVEN BETTER, IN ADVANCE (THIS IS CALLED PRO-FORMA INVOICING).

Whenever you set up a new customer, they will invariably ask for credit terms. Some customers, if they are big and powerful (like supermarkets for example) have standard credit terms and they are usually not very good towards their suppliers. In the worst-case scenario they might only pay you after 90 days! Other scenarios are 75 days, 60 days, 45 days and 30 days. You will also see "end of month +30" which essentially can extend payment to 60 days if they order on the 1st of the month!

They will also try on other awful practices such as early payment discounts. Unfortunately, they normally hold all the power and, consequently, the bargaining chips, and it's often a take it or leave it situation if you wish to trade with them.

However, when it comes to smaller customers, or foreign customers, you should always ask for pro-forma payment and hold on to that for as long as you can.

You should never… and I repeat… never, offer a credit facility to a customer you do not know, have never heard of and have not traded with. In fact, in my business, there have been some known scams of fake customers asking for goods.

Recently a friend of mine called me and asked my advice on a Scottish wholesaler who wanted to order 56 pallets from them with a total value of £60,000! There was no website, no information on them anywhere and what's more no customer would stock hold that amount of product! Remember, if it's too good to be true… it normally is. So please use your wits about you and err on the side of caution when it comes to trading.

BAD DEBTS

WHEN SOMEONE DOES NOT PAY YOU, THIS IS KNOWN AS A 'BAD DEBT.'
BAD DEBTS CAN DESTROY YOUR BUSINESS.

I learnt this the hard way early on, when my Australian distributor purchased £100k worth of stock and did not pay for it. I was emotionally involved at the time because they were related to one of my shareholders. The biggest mistake I made was handing over this huge amount of stock on the promise of payment, because I naively thought that the close connection to my shareholder would ensure some level of integrity. Boy was I wrong!

They paid about £20k of the money due, but the remainder (£80k) never materialized. They then had the audacity to copy the design of my brand and tell the market we had rebranded. The infringement of my brand was the straw the broke the camel's back. I had spent a lot of money registering trademarks around the world and felt that this was a wasted exercise if I could enforce my copyright. I also knew I was right and that the law was on my side and, therefore, the balance of probability was also tipped in my favour. So I did what I felt I had to do, and I litigated against them.

This was a painful and stressful period of the business and my life, and I had to personally loan the business my own money to ensure we did not collapse as we went under by £20k due to the bad debt initially. I also managed to put in place an overdraft facility with the bank which helped.

The only people that really won in this situation were the lawyers who made a sickening amount of money.

I VOWED, AFTER THAT MOMENT, TO NEVER HAVE A BAD DEBT AGAIN.

AND I NEVER HAVE.

There is one weapon in your arsenal that can help you here...

CREDIT INSURANCE

You can, in fact, insure your sales ledger. In other words, there are insurance companies that will pay you if a customer defaults on an invoice.

When you get a new customer, you ask them to fill in a credit form (sample in appendix). You then visit your online portal, enter the customer, and request a credit facility. The insurance company have access to every company, both here and abroad, and will issue you with an acceptance or a refusal based on the amount requested. For example, if my new customer is McJoe's Hamburger Joint, and McJoe's want to buy from me but request a £2000 credit facility, I will plug £2000 into the online portal. Once approved, I can safely trade with McJoe's, knowing the invoices are protected.

This can also be a great way to 'blame it on your insurance company.' In other words, everyone will be asking for credit terms from you, but you can always say it's not up to you... it's pending approval by the insurers.

I USE, AND WOULD RECOMMEND, EULER HERMES:
http://www.eulerhermes.com/

OVERDRAFT FACILITY

If you do find yourself skirting close to zero in your bank account, ask the bank for an overdraft facility. There will be some form filling to do but it can be well worth it. It is usually up to you do decide how much you want (£5,000, £10,000 etc) and this will normally be checked and approved by their credit departments. If you get rejected, ask them what is the maximum overdraft they will extend to you.

Remember to cancel it if you do not need it anymore, as some banks charge for having this facility in place.

INVOICE FINANCING

Invoice financing, also known as invoice discounting or invoice factoring, is where you have an invoice for goods you have sold, but you have not received payment yet for those goods. You take that invoice and a lender will lend you money (typically up to 80%) of the value of that invoice. They will charge interest and reclaim the loan when the invoice is paid off.

Invoice Factoring can be good as it helps you grow in line with your sales and is only a short term loan.

YOU HAVE TWO MAIN OPTIONS

BANKS:
Almost all banks invoice discount. The main disadvantage of using a bank is that they will take control of your entire sales ledger. In other words, they will ask that all of your customers pay into a bank account owned by the bank. This can be irritating if you already have a customer base and they already pay into your bank account. Also, they factor the entire ledger, as opposed to just one invoice.

ONLINE LENDERS:
With the power of crowd lending, there are some fabulous online lenders that will lend on the value of your invoice. I have used, and highly recommend, MarketInvoice, which I touched on briefly before. The way it works is that you post your invoice online, and lenders (really members of the public who have money) bid to lend you money. This creates a competitive auction-type environment,

and as a result, the interest you pay on the loan keeps going down until the auction closes. The great advantage is that you don't need to factor your entire sales ledger. If you just want to borrow the value of one invoice, you just upload one invoice.

By the way, if you are an investor, you can also make 10.65%[7] return by lending money to the platform.

FOR MORE INFO:
https://www.marketinvoice.com

WHEN YOU FACTOR AN INVOICE.

SIMPLE ECONOMICS (EXPLAINED SIMPLY)

If you don't come from a business background, it can be fairly daunting trying to comprehend margins, P & L, balance sheets, and percentages.

DON'T BE SCARED.

I didn't know any of it either, before I started my business, and now I'm writing a book. You must not shy away from it, and it is absolutely crucial that you take the time to digest it. You don't need to become an accountant, just understand a few basics and you'll be a whiz in no time. Take time to read and practice the formulas in this chapter. I guarantee you will end up using them everyday. And proper comprehension of margins and how to calculate them is how you determine if you make money or not.

My staff will tell you that I regularly give them pop quizzes on margins and percentages. In fact, I give this to everyone in my office – the marketing team, the graphic designers etc. That's because I believe in *creating* entrepreneurs, and I want everyone that works for me to be grounded in basic economics so that they leave my company ready to start their own business and live their own dream.

HANDY DEFINITIONS

COGS (COST OF GOODS):
This is the how much it costs you to buy your goods (if you are selling goods) and should include all landed and delivery costs.

RRP (RECOMMENDED RETAIL PRICE):
Also known as SRP (Suggested Retail Price). This is how much you sell your goods for.

GPM (GROSS PROFIT MARGIN):
Also known as Gross Margin. Expressed as a percentage. This is the difference between the sales price minus the cost of goods, divided by the sales price. To turn a figure into a percentage you need to multiply by 100, or just move the decimal point by two places. (ie, .50 is the same as 50%)

$$\text{GROSS PROFIT MARGIN} = \frac{\text{REVENUE} - \text{COGS}}{\text{REVENUE}}$$

NET PROFIT MARGIN:
Used to explain a company's pricing strategy after your operating costs. Also expressed as a percentage.

$$\text{NET PROFIT MARGIN} = \frac{\text{OPERATING INCOME}}{\text{NET SALES}}$$

VAT (VALUE ADDED TAX):
The standard level of VAT in the UK is 20%. However some items are zero rated, meaning they do not have any tax added to them.

TO RESEARCH WHETHER YOU NEED TO ADD VAT, VISIT:
https://www.gov.uk/guidance/rates-of-vat-on-different-goods-and-services

MARGINS EXPLAINED

AS A RULE...
THE HIGHER GROSS MARGIN FOR YOU, THE BETTER.

If you are in the business of buying and selling goods, it is generally a good idea to aim for a gross margin above 40%. That's because by the time you subtract all of your operating costs (wages, marketing, office rental etc), you are left with your net profit margin, basically your gross margin less all of your costs. That margin will obviously be less than 40% and could even be negative.

GETTING YOUR PRICING RIGHT

Running a profitable business is based on buying and selling at the right price.

SO WHAT YOU NEED TO FIRST DO IS AS FOLLOWS:

1. Understand what your Cost of Goods are (COGS). This means adding everything, including any import taxes, labels, packaging and delivery charges to give you your landed unit price.

2. Understand if your product is VATABLE or Zero Rated. This will affect your RRP (sales price). If someone says a price is net of VAT, it means that it is without the vat. For example, £1.80 is the RRP inclusive of VAT. The figure net of VAT is £1.50.

3. Have a rough idea of how much your product should sell for based on the existing market. Do your research.

Have an idea of what margins your retailers and wholesalers work on, (if you use or sell to either of them). For example, supermarkets tend to work on margins of between 40%-50%. Wholesalers work on a 28%-30% and they sell to small independents that tend to work on a 25% margin.

NOW THAT YOU KNOW THE ABOVE YOU ARE READY TO GET STARTED.

OPEN AN EXCEL SPREADSHEET AND COPY THE FOLLOWING:

STEP 1

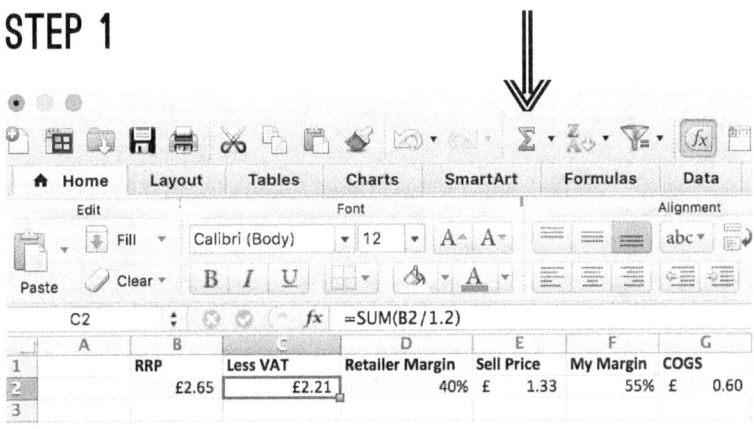

1. Type in RRP, LESS VAT, RETAILER MARGIN, SELL PRICE, MY MARGIN, COGS in Row 1.

2. In B2, type in your RRP (or what you think it should sell for). This is a price inclusive of VAT.

3. In C2, type in =SUM(B2/1.2) If you are familiar with excel you can use the shortcut button ∑ which can be found in the top row of the program. Dividing by 1.2 takes off 20% VAT from your number.

4. Next, in D2, first format the cell as a percentage cell by clicking the % button.

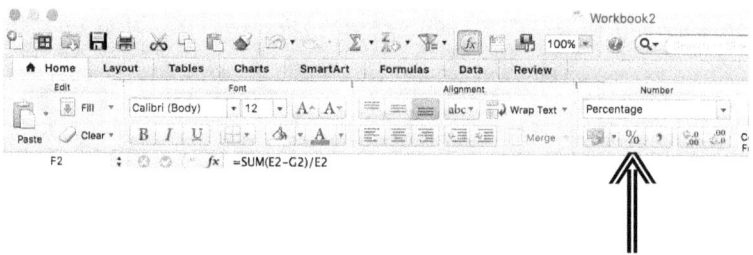

5. Enter the percent margin your retailer requires. I entered 40%, which is a common margin for major retailers like supermarkets.

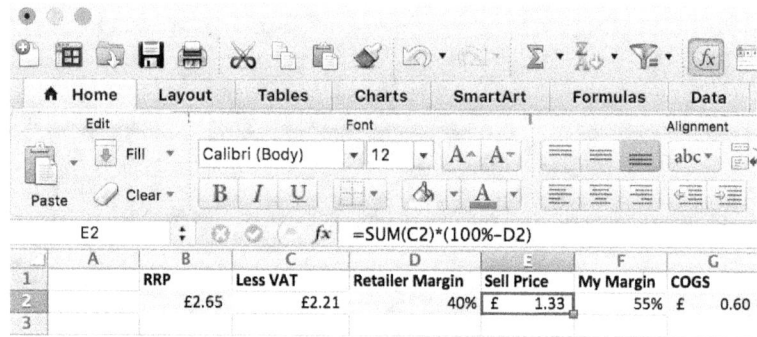

6. In E2, write the following: =SUM(C2)*(100%-D2)

What you are doing here is subtracting 40% from 100%, which gives you your margin, 60%. You are then calculating 60% of the net retail price, which gives you your sell price. If you change the margin or the RRP, you will see that E2 will change with it.

7. In G2 enter your Cost of Goods (COGS). Remember to have worked out your landed cost of goods.

8. In F2, first format the cell again by clicking the % symbol. Now type the following formula: =SUM (E2-G2)/E2.

This is the formula for working out your margin and is the sales price less the cost of goods, divided by the sales price.

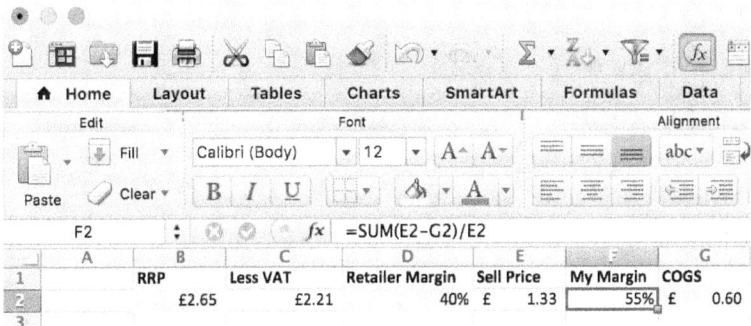

Where cells are highlighted yellow, you can change these figures and all other cells will repopulate. Now you can see what happens if you lower or raise the RRP, and also what happens if a customer requires a higher margin.

REMEMBER, YOU NEED TO AIM FOR A HIGH GROSS MARGIN, ABOVE 40% IS YOUR TARGET.

THAT IS HOW YOU CALCULATE WHAT PRICE YOU SHOULD SELL AT.

FIVE USEFUL FORMULAS EVERY ENTREPRENEUR SHOULD KNOW

REMOVING VAT:
DIVIDE BY 1.2.

For example:
£1.50 / 1.2 = £1.25 (PRICE NET OF VAT)

ADDING VAT:
MULTIPLY BY 1.2.

For example:
£1.50*1.2 = £1.80 (PRICE INC OF VAT)

CALCULATE GROSS MARGIN (GM):
REVENUE (R) MINUS COST OF GOODS (COGS) DIVIDED BY REVENUE (R).

For example, I sell my widget for £2.99 (R). My Cost of goods is £1.35 (COGS). So my equation would look like this:

$$GM = \frac{R - COGS}{R} \implies \frac{£2.99 - £1.35}{£2.99} = .54\ (54\%)$$

CALCULATE NET MARGIN (NM):
OPERATING INCOME (OI) DIVIDED BY NET SALES (NS)

For example, my operating income is £200,000 (OI). My net income is £850,000, therefore:

$$NM = \frac{OI}{NS} \implies \frac{£200,000}{£850,000} = .23\ (23\%)$$

ADDING A PERCENTAGE TO A NUMBER:
SUBTRACT THE PERCENTAGE FROM 100%. TAKE YOUR NUMBER AND THEN DIVIDE IT BY THE LEFTOVER PERCENTAGE.

For example, to add 40% to 1.50, you subtract 40% from 100% which equals 60%. Then you take £1.50 and divide by .60.

$$\frac{£1.50}{100\% - 40\%} = £2.50$$

Another example: I want to sell my widget for 25% more than my cost of goods. My cost of goods is .60p, so:

$$\frac{£.60}{100\% - 25\%} = £.80$$

OKAY...
POP QUIZ

These are questions we have to work out in our business all the time. Grab a piece of paper and work out the following. Answers in the appendix!

1. You are selling your widget to Homebase. They require a 45% margin. Your RRP is £4.99 inclusive of VAT. Net of VAT, calculate the price you should sell to them.

2. It costs you £.43p to manufacture your widget. If you sell to your customer at £1.05, what is your Gross Profit Margin?

3. You wish to add 33% to your cost of goods, which is £4.99. What is the new price?

4. BONUS: The RRP of my widget is £3.49 inc VAT. My retailer takes 25% margin off the RRP net of VAT. They buy from the wholesaler who takes 28%. My cost of goods is £1.05. What price does the retailer buy from the wholesaler, the wholesaler buy from me, and what is my margin?

Now try a few scenarios using your actual figures. I promise that you'll need all of these formulas, so study these well!

CHECK YOUR ANSWERS ON PAGE 170... NO CHEATING!

UNDERSTANDING PROFIT & LOSS

If you use XERO, you can view your P & L (Profit and Loss) sheet at any time. It's actually quite easy to read once you get the hang of it.

On the following page I have printed out a sample Profit & Loss sheet. Apart from looking fairly straightforward, I've annotated it with some notes.

On the page after I am going to show you how to read the P & L in terms of gross margin and net margin as expressed in a percentage. So next time you decide to go on Dragon's Den you'll be able to take the grilling.

A. YOUR TOTAL TURNOVER/SALES

B. YOUR TOTAL COST OF GOODS (COGS)

(A) - (B) = GROSS PROFIT (GP)

C. OPERATING EXPENSES

GROSS PROFIT - (C) = NET PROFIT

PROFIT & LOSS SHEET EXAMPLE

YEAR TO DATE

	FEB-16	JAN-16	DEC-15	YTD
INCOME				
Other Revenue	-	-	115	3,063
Sales	37,342	129,016	94,615	1,993,734
TOTAL INCOME	37,342	129,016	94,615	1,996,797
LESS COST OF SALES				
Direct Expenses	340	201,152	65,554	1,668,498
Postage, Freight & Courier	410	6,061	7,644	146,416
Warehouse/Storage	62	5,071	4,248	56,352
TOTAL COST OF SALES	812	212,284	77,446	1,871,267
GROSS PROFIT	36,530	83,268	17,168	125,530
PLUS OTHER INCOME				
Discounts	(1,167)	(3,763)	(5,142)	(16,794)
TOTAL OTHER INCOME	(1,167)	(3,763)	(5,142)	(16,794)
LESS OPERATING EXPENSES				
Advertising & Marketing	510	14,151	3,879	277,447
Agents Commissions	128	141	243	3,616
Audit & Accountancy Fees	-	6,000	-	10,263
Bank Fees	20	37	156	1,598
Charitable & Political Donations	-	-	1,500	7,600
Cleaning	-	67	80	853
Consulting	3,800	2,753	6,595	35,100
Employers National Insurance	-	4,632	4,573	55,407
Entertainment - 100% Business	-	23	-	1,162
Foreign Currency Gains & Loses	(433)	1,159	2,243	5,691
General Expenses	145	158	88	1,929
Insurance	265	365	365	7,348
Interest Paid	-	185	189	2,200
IT Software & Consumables	119	198	255	2,080
Legal Expenses	-	-	-	1,476
Light, Power, Heating	128	-	-	455
Motor Vehicle Expenses	-	-	-	253
Printing & Stationery	66	-	19	997
Rates	-	500	500	5,000
Rent	2,691	2,691	2,691	28,709
Salaries	5,833	12,152	10,051	124,777
Staff Entertainment	84	71	265	1,005
Staff Training	-	-	-	1,150
Telephone & Internet	52	270	287	3,639
Travel - National	81	124	65	3,491
TOTAL OPERATING EXPENSES	13,489	45,676	34,043	583,247
NET PROFIT	21,874	(132,707)	(22,018)	(474,510)

BALANCE SHEET

On the following page is a sample balance sheet which you can also print out from XERO. A balance sheet very simply shows you your net assets. It is a simple way of understanding your company's net assets (ie what it is worth) It is calculated thus:

ASSETS - LIABILITIES = NET ASSETS

ASSETS:

are all the things you have that are worth money... money in the bank, money due to you, property, machinery, and stock. You add them all together and this gives you your total assets.

LIABILITIES:

are all the thing you owe... all of the bills on your ledger, loans, perhaps VAT. You add all of these together and this gives you your total liabilities.

Giving Tree Ventures Ltd
As at 30 September 2018

	30 Sep 2018
Assets	
Bank	
Giving Tree (Natwest)	1,423
Giving Tree Ventures (LTSB)	6
Total Bank	**1,428**
Current Assets	
Accounts Receivable	14,301 [1]
Inventory Asset	11,488
Stock - Finished Goods	1,138
Stock - Raw Materials	97,203
Stock at Hand	266
Total Current Assets	**124,396**
Fixed Assets	
Buildings	2,574
Leasehold Improvements	31
Motor Vehicles	1,920
Office Equipment	1,637
Plant & Machinery	10,051
Less Accumulated Depreciation on Plant and Machinery	(3,618)
Total Fixed Assets	**12,596**
Total Assets	**138,420**
Liabilities	
Current Liabilities	
Accounts Payable	29,286 [1]
Accruals	1,500
Directors' Loan Account	2,500
PAYE Payable	(49)
Rounding	(240)
Suspense	(36)
VAT	(145)
Total Current Liabilities	**32,816**
Non-Current Liabilities	
Loan	104,583
Total Non-Current Liabilities	**104,583**
Total Liabilities	**137,399**
Net Assets	**1,021**
Equity	
Capital - x,xxx Ordinary Shares	100
Current Year Earnings	31,718

OUTSOURCING

AS ENTREPRENEURS, THE TEMPTATION IS TO DO EVERYTHING OURSELVES.

However, businesses are much more efficient when some elements are outsourced.

One of the main advantages of outsourcing is that you do not require any capital outlay (ie, the money) to fund the purchasing of equipment and machinery. Assets cost money. And then they cost more money to run and staff.

Some of the biggest brands in the world are built entirely on outsourcing and have minimal assets. Many .com businesses are merely interfaces: Instagram, Twitter, Facebook, Uber. Yes they require people to code, but Uber doesn't own any taxis, and Instragram doesn't own any cameras.

Similarly, many high street brands as you know them do not own the machinery behind the brands. It's fair to say that a large percentage use co-packers and third party factories in India or Asia to make their goods.

THE VALUE OF A BRAND, IS IN THE BRAND ITSELF.

Think about that. Nike, Coke, Apple, GAP – the value of the brand is the brand itself. When you buy a brand, you are buying on the promise and expectation of that brand delivering something to you. When companies are sold or traded, the value is placed in the brand equity almost more than companies with assets. Think about a house that you buy. That house has finite value, depending on the market. The prices of houses go up and down relative to the market. But a brand that has no assets can have an exponential value that really defies any logic. We'll talk more about valuations later.

In my own business, everything is outsourced. In fact, here's a list of everything I outsource to other people:

FARMERS PICK COCONUTS AND DELIVER THEM TO FACTORIES

FACTORIES CUT OPEN, DRAIN, FILTER AND PACK THE COCONUT WATER

A SHIPPING COMPANY SHIPS THE GOODS IN A SEA CONTAINER

A HAULIER PICKS UP THE GOODS AND DRIVES THEM TO MY WAREHOUSE

MY WAREHOUSE, OWNED BY A THIRD PARTY, RECEIVE AND STORE THE GOODS

WHEN I RECEIVE AN ORDER, WE SEND IT TO THE WAREHOUSE AND A TRUCK DELIVERS THE GOODS TO THE CUSTOMER

And we don't own any of the above. In fact, we are just in an office in London making sure everything goes smoothly. We don't own any equipment, any trucks, and warehouses or any factories. We could be on a beach in Jamaica with a laptop and still run the business.

THAT'S CALLED OUTSOURCING.

Now look at the opposite. Imagine you make wine and own a vineyard. You have to plant the trees, harvest the grapes, crush the grapes, ferment the juice, buy the machines, run the machines, clean the machines, pay for parts, bottle the wine, sell the wine and distribute the wine. Whilst it might be fun making wine... it's also labour intensive and, what's more, very expensive to fund the machinery behind it.

When I first started CHI, I outsourced the design via a company called elance (it's now called upwork), which I have previously mentioned: https://www.upwork.com/

You can literally find anyone to do anything for you – designers, animators, video makers, researchers, business plan writers, lawyers... you name it.

And as you grow, you can outsource anything you need to run your business.

There are even virtual offices, virtual telephone numbers and virtual assistants. So you can have the appearance of large business without the cost of one.

If you are selling goods, here are some of the things I recommend you outsource:

MANUFACTURE

ALL DESIGN (BRANDING, ADS ETC)

WAREHOUSING

LOGISTICS

E-COMMERCE

TIME MANAGEMENT

Running a business can be labour intensive. If you are in the restaurant or retail trade, you might find you need to be there all the time, every day, seven days a week. That doesn't leave time for much else: family, exercise, or friends. After all, what are we working for? More money? More time? Do we want to work to be able to retire and live in a big house in Spain? Are we hoping that by working hard now, one day we will be happy?

NEWS FLASH

HAPPINESS IS THE JOURNEY, **NOT THE DESTINATION!**

Wouldn't it be better if you *made time* now for everything that was important in your life?

TIME IS A FUNNY OLD THING.

We all complain we don't have enough of it. But time is out there for the taking. It's just up to you how you use it. And most of us do not use it very well. Sometimes we truly are very busy for small patches, but most of the time we are just pretending that we don't have enough time. We like to tell people how busy we are, that we just don't 'have any time'. If you really truly look at your day and how you spend every minute, do you *really* not have any time?

The whole notion of not having enough time is what I referred to earlier in the book as a 'racket'. If you have read any books on psychology you may be familiar with transactional analysis and the idea of rackets.

WIKI DEFINES RACKETS THIS WAY:
"A racket is then a set of behaviours which originate from the childhood script rather than in here-and-now full Adult thinking, which (1) are employed as a way to manipulate the environment to match the script rather than to actually solve the problem, and (2) whose covert goal is not so much to solve the problem, as to experience these racket feelings and feel internally justified in experiencing them."

Not having enough time is one of your impediments to success. So next time you put off doing something, recognise if the excuse you are making is just fulfilling your script.

As an entrepreneur, I am always ready to deal with something in my business, 24 hours a day, 7 days a week, should it arise.

Building a successful business is great. But don't neglect your life or your family. If you have successfully outsourced elements of your business, you will find that your working day will be easy and balanced and you will be able to make time for other things.

If today were you last day on earth, where would you be and what would you be doing? I'll bet you would not be in your office in front of your computer nor would your face be buried in social media. I'd venture a guess that you'd be at home with your loved ones, playing and being present in the moment.

WHY NOT TRY TO LIVE EVERYDAY AS IF IT WERE YOU LAST?

WHAT IS SUCCESS?

LET ME ASK YOU A QUESTION.

What does success look like to you?

Is success measured by the turnover of your business? By making more money than your competitor? Is it selling your business for £50 million.

Is success having a mansion, a swimming pool, a Bentley, or staff to wait on you? Is success having a villa in Greece?

WHAT HAPPENS WHEN YOU GET ALL YOU DREAM OF? WHAT THEN?

If you get it all, and you have fulfilled your definition of success… will you be happy? Will you be truly content? Will you still feel like there's something still missing that you can't quite put your finger on?

There is nothing wrong with having these things or aspiring to have them in your life. We all enjoy surface pleasure and there is no doubting it makes our lives more comfortable.

Earlier in the book I mentioned Robert Waldinger's study on happiness. If you didn't yet watch the video, please take a moment and watch it now:

https://www.ted.com/talks/robert_waldinger_what_makes_a_good_life_lessons_from_the_longest_study_on_happiness?language=en

PUTTING TOGETHER THE JIGSAW OF YOUR BUSINESS SO IT CAN RUN EFFORTLESSLY

Here's a bit of checklist for you to think about based on some of the hints and tricks from the previous chapters:

DO SOME MARKET RESEARCH

DESIGN YOUR BRAND

SOURCE YOUR GOODS

REGISTER YOUR TRADEMARK IN UK OR EU

REGISTER YOUR LTD COMPANY THROUGH COMPANIES HOUSE

PUT TOGETHER A BUSINESS PLAN

RAISE FINANCE

SUBSCRIBE TO XERO

FIGURE OUR YOUR PRICING AND YOUR GROSS PROFIT MARGIN

NEGOTIATE LONG CREDIT TERMS WITH YOUR SUPPLIERS, AND SHORT CREDIT TERMS WITH YOUR CUSTOMERS TO ENSURE YOU GET PAID QUICKLY AND YOU DON'T HAVE TO PAY YOUR BILLS STRAIGHT AWAY

OUTSOURCE LOGISTICS, WAREHOUSING, & MANUFACTURING

STAY ON TOP OF YOUR DAILY BOOKKEEPING

IF NEED BY, FACTOR YOUR INVOICES (BORROW AGAINST THE VALUE)

MANAGE YOUR TIME WELL AND FIND A PLACE FOR EXERCISE AND FAMILY

IMPORT/EXPORT

At some point you may wish to export your goods to other countries. There are some things you need to know about exporting.

Buyers from other countries tend to buy ex-works. This means that they collect from your UK or local warehouse. They pay for all the costs of delivering those goods to their own warehouse and any import duty and local taxes.

If you are trading in the EU, there are currently free trade agreements in place, meaning that goods can circulate freely across member states.

Non-EU member states might have duty/taxes to pay on the goods as they enter the country. Others might have things like sugar taxes.

When you are selling to a foreign distributor, remember that their costs are going to be a lot higher than if you were selling to a UK company, so you will have to take a hit on your margins.

MY ADVICE IS DON'T BE GREEDY.

The strategy here should be in brand building. If you start off with prices that are too high you will scare off your buyer. A 10-15% margin is completely acceptable. Obviously, a hgher margin, the better, but it all depends on your cost of goods and what you feel the buyer can sell for given their additional costs. You don't want them to be selling at such a high RRP that your goods don't sell in their country.

Remember, it is difficult to recoup money from overseas companies, so act with caution and ask for pro-forma payment unless you have insured your customer through your insurance policy (see chapter on credit insurance).

Typically, you may also meet some 'agents' along the way who promise to sell to distributors. An agent will be a middleman. Consequently, there will be an added margin in between you and the distributor. I recommend working directly with distributors. You are only adding a layer of complication and unwanted margin onto your product, which will have an effect on the retail price of your goods in the buyer's country. Cut out middlemen if you can.

Some customers may ask you for some documents. Normally your shipper can take care of these. However, in some instances, you may need to create them.

Typically, some certificates you may need to create will be:

EUR1 CERTIFICATE (THROUGH LONDON CHAMBER OF COMMERCE)

CERTIFICATE OF ORIGIN (THROUGH LONDON CHAMBER OF COMMERCE)

ARAB CERTIFICATE OF ORIGIN (THROUGH LONDON CHAMBER OF COMMERCE AND LOCALIZED BY LOCAL EMBASSY)

HEALTH CERTIFICATE/ CERTIFICATE OF FREE SALE (ISSUED BY THE RURAL PAYMENTS AGENCY)

COMMERCIAL INVOICE (YOU CAN MAKE THIS)

PACKING LIST (YOU CAN MAKE THIS, YOU JUST NEEDS WEIGHTS AND VOLUMES OF YOUR GOODS)

CONTACTS:

London Chamber of Commerce (LCC):
http://www.londonchamber.co.uk/

Rural Payments Agency (RPA)
https://www.gov.uk/government/organisations/rural-payments-agency

The UKTI (UK Trade and investment) are also extremely helpful when it comes to export and have offices in almost every country. Worth connecting with your local office:

https://www.gov.uk/government/publications/ukti-teams-in-the-english-regions/ukti-london-helping-companies-export-and-grow-overseas

TRADE FAIRS

Trade fairs can be a great way to meet foreign distributors. The UK holds many trade fairs throughout the year and there are some great ones in Europe and the Middle East specific to your industry.

Don't spend too much money on your stand. You'll get a zillion enquiries, and less than 1% will materialize into tangible sales. If you get one sale from a trade fair that pays for your stand, consider it a result! Also, you are there to form relationships that will pay off over time. Often I have met the same distributors at trade fairs and only started working with them a year or two later.

You will need to get someone to build your stand. There are some great mobile stands out there that pack easily into a wheeled box and start from only £400. Just Google "Exhibition pop up stand". They are all much of a muchness, and mainly printers who buy in the blank stand – so don't stress too much over the vast array of choices out there.

Trade fairs are exhausting and very costly. Target which shows you want to exhibit at. It may be a good idea to visit it first to see if it's something for you.

CONSUMER FAIRS

A consumer fair is targeted at end to end customers. Usually you can sell at these fairs. There is an endless array of consumer fairs too. I strongly advise you to pick focused consumer fairs specific to your category. You'll find the customer base is much more receptive to your business.

HS CODES

When it comes to importing your goods, the amount of tax you will pay depends on your Tariff Code. Different goods attract different rates of tax.
Your first port of call should be the online Tariff Checker:
https://www.gov.uk/trade-tariff

It's a fairly confusing system, so if you get stuck, there is a helpline you can call to help classify your goods: 0300 200 3700

You may also want to consider getting a BTI (Binding Tariff Information), which means the government makes a firm decision about the type and classification of your goods for import tax purposes.
https://www.gov.uk/government/publications/notice-600-classifying-your-imports-or-exports/notice-600-classifying-your-imports-or-exports

GLOSSARY OF SHIPPING TERMS

When you import or export your goods, there are a number of different ways to buy or sell. Each one has an impact on your costs. Below I am covering the main ones you are likely to encounter.

FOB (FREE ON BOARD):
If you buy FOB, it means your goods are send as far as the portal. All onward costs from the port have to be paid for by the buyer.

EXW (EXWORKS):
This means buyer or seller collects from the factory. All onward costs (to port and beyond) the buyer must cover.

BOL (BILL-OF-LADING):

This is a binding contract (like a receipt) between the shipper and the freight carrier. It will specifiy the destination and details of the shipment.

CIF (COST, INSURANCE, FREIGHT):

This is a delivered cost to the port in the destination country, but onward transport from the port to the warehouse and also and taxes and clearance charges must be paid for by the buyer.

DDP (DELIVERY, DUTY PAID):

This is a fully delivered cost to the buyer's warehouse. Including, freight, duty, clearance and onward delivery.

CONSOLIDATION:

This is the act of consolidating goods from different origin points. For example, let's say your buyer is shipping five products from different brand owners. He will need to consolidate his goods together.

LTL (LESS THAN A TRUCKLOAD):

When you are not shipping full truckloads, (just pallets), this is known as an LTL shipment.

FTL (FULL TRUCK LOAD):

When you fill a truck with goods, this is know as a FTL.

FCL (FULL CONTAINER LOAD):

When you ship a full container, this is known as FCL.

LCL (LESS THAN CONTAINER LOAD):

Likewise, when you just ship pallets on a container, your goods will ship with other goods, and this is known as an LCL.

REEFER:
This is a refrigerated container which can be either chilled or frozen.

20FCL, 40FCL:
Containers come in different sizes – this refers to the capacity of the container. Normally a 20FCL can hold 10 pallets and a 40FCL can hold 20 pallets (but check with your supplier because pallet sizes can vary).

DEMURRAGE:
This is a system of penalty charges imposed if goods are held for longer than normal (for example if they get stuck at port due to customs issues)

PALLET:
This is the wooden base holding goods. The UK operates a CHEP (blue) pallet system ensuring all pallets get returned to source and reused.

SHIPPER/CONSIGNOR:
This is the company or individual that sends the freight.

CONSIGNEE:
This is the company or individual receiving the freight.

NETWORKING

It goes without saying that getting out and networking is important. It's easy to get stopped by fear. In turn, it's easy to stay home and not step out of your comfort zone.

Try to go to as many events as you can. Next time you do, find someone else who is by themselves and simply introduce yourself. I guarantee they are feeling equally as insecure as you are. Don't spend too long, exchange cards, and then continue to mingle.

Also, don't be afraid to reach out to strangers in your industry. I have done this all my life and continue to do this on a regular basis.

Last week I bumped into Tim Burton (Director of BeetleJuice, Charlie and the Chocolate Factory and many more amazing movies). It should be noted I don't know him and have never met him.

He was at the cinema with his kids, and as the movie finished I spotted him. I knew I had one opportunity, so as we were leaving, I said "Wasn't as good as Edward Scissorhands." This broke the ice and we chatted for a few minutes and then I asked if I could send him a project.

Only last week I reached out (cold) to half a dozen CEOs of some of the biggest snack companies in the UK. I specifically wrote down all the companies I felt had synergy with my snacks company, researched who the CEOs were, dug hard on Google and managed to find their email addresses. Two responded. Two meetings scheduled.

When I thought about selling CHI, I thought about the potential buyers for my company, and discovered the billion dollar Japanese company Suntory. I had one email address. I wrote off this person.

I heard nothing for several months.

Then, out of the blue, I received an email from the CEO of Lucozade/Ribena in the UK (owned by Suntory) following up with me. The conversation turned into a meeting.

ASK AND YOU SHALL RECEIVE

It goes without saying that you cannot win the lottery if you don't actually buy a ticket. Likewise, if you don't ask, you cannot get. Most of us get stopped before the 'asking' bit, usually out of fear, or out of an inability to step out of our comfort zone.

Just yesterday one of my employees was tasked with contacting food chains. She jumped on to Linked In and happened upon the CEO of a Thai Chain in London. She decided to send him an email saying he needed raw coconut water. He wrote back and said "I agree".

There are two lessons to be learnt here. First, you must try. If you try, the outcome will be success or failure. If you do not try, the only outcome is no outcome, and with no outcome and no result, that is a lost opportunity and a potential fail.

SECOND, SOMETIMES IT PAYS TO GO TO THE TOP.

My theory about this is as follows: CEOs, business owners and entrepreneurs care passionately about their business. Employees who earn a monthly paycheck often do not carry that same passion and therefore will be less engaged with the outcome of certain decisions. Therefore when you contact someone who has no emotional attachment to the business, the general response is a 'fob off'. Ultimately most people want to reduce their work load. So when they receive an unsolicited email from someone they do not know, trying to sell them something, they will hit the delete button.

However, someone that has emotional attachment to their business, cares more about every aspect of it; the quality of their products, the brand, the image etc.

I have told you I recently emailed the CEOs of about 6 top snack companies. Two of them responded. That's a 33% success rate which made the cold calls totally worth it.

Having been on the receiving end of many cold calls and emails, some I have deleted or ignored, but many I have engaged with and ended up purchasing from or doing some other business with.

The lesson comes back to a fundamental notion, which is the need to 'take action' in every aspect of your business. Remember that thought leads to intention, and intention leads to action.

WITHOUT ACTION
NOTHING WILL MATERIALIZE.

VALUATIONS

Facebook is a great example of this. Before Facebook had any advertising whatsoever, it was just a social network. The first major investment came from Microsoft in 2007, who purchased a 1.6% share of the company for $240m, at a valuation of $15 billion! This was before it was even making any money. As a side note, when FB floated (ie, went public) in 2012, the valuation was $102 billion. As of 2015, Facebook's annual revenue is a staggering $17.928 billion per year with a net income of $3.6 billion.[8]

THE TEN RULES OF

LESSON 1

Money. You need it. You really do. If you want to launch a business you need capital. Otherwise you'll spend the majority of your time underfunded, looking for money. How do you get it? A good idea, a good business plan and the shameless drive to ask every person you've met and their close to home.

LESSON 2

Cash flow is king. It's something you won't appreciate until you've run a business. If you make a 10,000 units of your widget, and you pay up front, and it takes you 6 months to sell your widget, and you need to make more widgets in 3 months, your money is going

GOLDEN BUSINESS

out quicker then it's coming in. That's a problem for underfunded companies. It's the reason many companies, including Innocent, almost went bust as a victim of their own success.

Solutions: negotiate lengthy credit terms for when you buy, and short credit terms for when you sell. Borrow money against your invoices , EFG loans. But be weary. Cash flow can destroy you.

LESSON 3

Credit insurance. If there's one thing I learnt when I didn't get paid £100,000, is that I would never ever let that happen again. Insure your sales ledger, and do not offer credit to anyone you cannot insure. Otherwise they should pay upfront.

LESSON 4

What is your brand? You have to have a strong, consistent and creative brand. If you're not creative, hire someone. 95% of purchases are made on impulse on the spot and based on packaging. Be bold, take risks and think outside of the coconut.

LESSON 5

What is your product? Whatever it is, now that someone bought it on impulse, you better make damn sure that you can back it up by quality. Strive for the best ingredients, the best raw material – innovate in your space. Make it different. Make it better. You owe it to yourself... you owe it to the world.

LESSON 6

Manage your money yourself. Do your own bookkeeping, your invoicing, your purchasing, your payments. If you read the previous chapters, you'll know. I use an amazing program called XERO – and it's allowed me to understand how to read spreadsheets, profit and loss, balance sheets, and gives me an intimate understanding of the economics of my business. It's not as hard as you think, and it's fun, believe it or not.

LESSON 7

Understand what margins are. And because I really want you to understand—here's a formula if you've skipped a chapter. Your gross margin is calculated by the sale price minus the cost of goods divided by the sale price. That one's for free, please write it down. It's super important and there might be another test at the end of this lesson.

LESSON 8

Don't be greedy. A smaller piece of a bigger pie is worth more than a bigger piece of a smaller pie. You need people and money to grow. Preferably people with money. And people with money want shares in your company.

LESSON 9

Have an exit plan. Unless you want to work your whole life, which is fine too. Otherwise, think about where you want to be in 3 years and how you're gonna achieve it.

LESSON 10

Ask and you shall receive. With everything. Network and reach out to people, even people at the top. Some of the people I've had coffee with include the founder of GU, the founder of Coffee republic and the founder of Phones for you. The latter sold his company for over a billion pounds and is the 16th richest man in Britain. All through networking or reaching out.

AND FINALLY, A BONUS LESSON...

LESSON 11

Give back. Give to those less fortunate than you. As we speak we've just built a well in India for a community that had no access to clean water. It feels much better to give than to receive... I promise you. So whether it's for selfish reasons, vanity, or public perception, it doesn't really matter. What matters is the end result and how it helps those people.

TEN GOLDEN RULES OF MAKING YOUR IDEA A REALITY

LESSON 1

You need a great idea. It's obvious, I know. But you see, whilst I want to tell you to follow your instincts, follow your dreams and build it regardless of what people say, I also want to tell you that you need some common sense. Here's the questions you need to ask yourself.

Has it been done before? If it has, you will find greater barriers to entry and reluctance when you launch.

If it has been done before, can you do it better? Or can you do it different? Can you innovate in a well established category? Otherwise why bother creating a 'me too' product. It's boring and probably won't last.

Is it scalable? Why sell your product in a market on a Sunday when you have the world at your fingertips? If it's ready for the world, be sure you can scale it up. Dare to dream big.

Finally, here is the most important question you need to ask yourself. Do you have what it takes to commit and take action?

I'm going to answer that question for you. Yes. You do. Guess what? Every one has it. It's not magic. It's something far simpler than that. Ready?....

THE ABILITY TO TAKE ACTION.

You might be saying "easier said than done, Jonathan."

No. You can do it. Here's how.

LESSON 2

First, there's a little thing I like to call "integrity." Integrity is saying what you do and doing what you say. In other words, if you tell me you have bought tickets to see Matilda (great show by the way), and you tell me the tickets are £150 and non-refundable, and I tell you I'm going to attend, and I don't attend, that is NOT having integrity.

Now take that and apply it to the small things we say we are going to do but never do… go to the gym, eat less sweets, be romantic, write a thank you to a present. Think about how we make promises, hundreds of promises, only to break them. Integrity is saying what you are going to do, and then taking action consistent with what you have said. Without integrity you cannot take action. Without action you cannot achieve. Without achievement you cannot succeed.

In 1776 America made a 'declaration of independence." They weren't yet independent. They just declared it. Guess what? They then fought, passed a bill and took action consistent with the declaration.

I'm going to get a little philosophical here so bare with me. There are three levels of reality. What you think, what you say, and what you do.

We all have that inner voice in our heads. You know the one I'm talking about? The one judging and criticizing and commenting right now? It's generally never a coach, is it. In fact, it's pretty miserable and pretty negative. You can't do this. She hates me. I'm a failure. I'm angry. I'm upset. Life is meaningless. I cannot succeed. It's too hard.

If you listen to that voice, life pretty much sucks.

Guess what? I'm here to tell you, that that voice is not real. It's just a voice. It is full of sound and fury, signifying nothing.

What you say. Well, that's the first step to creating reaility. You verbalise something. "I am going to go the park on Sunday. I am going to bulk up and become a muscle god by going to the gym three times a week." You can say it... But if you don't do it, it is not real, and you have failed and you will never be a muscle god.

Integrity. Be your word. Because if you say it, you have to take action consistent with your word. If you commit verbally to going to the gym 3 times a week... go!

It's really quite simple! There's no magic to success. There is only action.

LESSON 3

The power of the word 'no.'

Don't get stopped by it. Likewise, don't be afraid to say it.

LESSON 4

Listen to those around you... but also, trust your instinct and don't listen to those around you. Might sound like a contradiction but here's the thing...

Your instinct is normally right. Even when those around you think you are wrong, or crazy. Trust your instinct. That's how lights were given electricity, rockets were built, planes have flown and bridges built. Every idea began with a crazy person that no one believed but who had the vision and self belief to push when everyone said pull.

LESSON 5

Pick yourself up when you get knocked.

Dwell on your failure, mourn your loss... just for a day, then get over it, and get over it quickly. Failure is an integral part of succeeding. Edison made 1000 unsuccessful attempts at inventing the light bulb. Vincent Van Gogh sold, during his lifetime.. wait for it.... 1 painting!

LESSON 6

Every coconut has a silver lining. When you do fail, which you will, how can you take that negative and turn it into a positive. Use it to motivate and inspire yourself and others. Be better. Be bigger. Or go home.

LESSON 7

Don't wait for the cow to back into your hands to milk it. Go into the field and milk the cow. And don't rely on anyone else to milk it either. You have to get your hands on the teat, and milk. Pick up the phone, send an email, and when you are done, do it again, and again and again.

YOU CAN'T WIN THE LOTTERY IF YOU DON'T BUY THE TICKET.

LESSON 7

DON'T BE AFRAID AND DON'T LIVE YOUR LIFE IN FEAR.

Fear, unless you have a gun pointed to your head, is not real. Fear is manufactured by your mind. Remember that inner voice I mentioned? Well fear is a manifestation of that inner voice. It's there to sabotage you. Don't let it win. Because as easily as you made fear appear in your life... you can make it disappear.

LESSON 8

FIND YOUR

YOU DO NEED TO WORK, BUT DON'T NEED TO BE A WORKAHOLIC.

You also need to live. After all, once you have made all the money you want, bought the house of your dreams, a large yacht, perhaps a tropical island... then what? Will you really be happy? If it were the last day of your life, what would you do, who would you want to see? I'd spend it with my kids and family. Why not live every day as if it were your last. Don't have regrets.

Have a hobby, go the gym, make time for yourself and your family. Switch off. Stay fit, and then do it all again tomorrow.

LESSON 9

Visualise what you want in the world – tell the universe. Declare it. But then recognize when the universe presents opportunities to you. It will give you an open door. But you have to walk through it.

Success is that perfect balance of luck, talent and taking action.

BALANCE.

LESSON 10

Love hard, be present. Put down your iphone and engage with the world around you.

CASE STUDY

SAHAR HASHEMI, COFFEE REPUBLIC

THE CHALLENGE WAS GETTING PEOPLE TO TASTE IT: TO BE "CONVERTED"

WHAT WAS YOUR LIGHT BULB MOMENT IN COMING UP WITH YOUR BUSINESS?

My light bulb moment was I went to New York and I had a skinny latte for the first time, and I'm always on some sort of a weird diet so I couldn't believe you could get skinny lattés and that was sort of the moment. And it wasn't really a lightbulb, but then I went and told my brother how great they were and how can we get to have them in London and he said we should start it and that's when it was the light bulb moment when my brother got the light bulb. After I complained to him that we didn't have skinny lattés in the UK.

HOW DID YOU COME UP WITH THE NAME?

Well we wanted the name to be all about coffee, "coffee country world". We didn't know what to call it. We went and checked all the white pages in the library to get any ideas we could from American bars, then suddenly I said to my brother what about coffee republic? Probably being inspired by banana republic and he said yep that's the name.

HOW DID YOU RAISE FINANCE?

We went to 40 banks and we met 20 bank managers. 19 of them said they will never give us a loan and finally the 20th bank manager, who somehow had to give us a loan, gave us a bank loan for £90,000 and we had it guaranteed under the small firms loans guarantee scheme which is the pre decessor to the enterprise finance scheme so we would have never done it without that scheme which guaranteed our bank loan.

WHAT WAS THE BIGGEST CHALLENGE YOU FACED WHEN STARTING UP?

The biggest challenge we faced was basically no one coming in. No one knew what skinny lattes were, macchiatos or iced coffees, so it was about educating people and people just going and having horrible coffee in those old school style sandwich bars. So the challenge was getting people to taste it; to be "converted" is the word we used. So we used to kind of say what we wanted to convert our customers, and that was getting people to come through the door and we tried everything there was. Every single marketing thing you can get from freebies to loyalty cards and deliveries to try and get people through the door.

WHAT WERE SOME OF THE BIGGEST MISTAKES YOU MADE ALONG THE WAY AND WHAT DID YOU LEARN FROM THEM?

I think one of the biggest mistakes we made along the way was thinking that when you are a big company you have to act big and you have to lose all that passion you had in the beginning. We thought companies grow up and acquire this prestige. We have learnt that actually is not the case. However much along a time line a company comes, you still need to have that passion and that customer focus that you had in the beginning and we thought, as the company got bigger, you should just give it to professionals to run, and that passion is worthless in a big company, in a mature company, and we were very wrong about that. So if I could go back in time, I would keep myself in there, get a great team that are just as passionate as me and continue the business.

When we had cash flow problems, I was lucky that my brother (my co-founder and partner), was very good at the finances, so I remember when we did the cash flow projection, he said what's the worst case scenario, and I told him, what if no one comes in this scenario, and he said well lets double the worst case scenario. I remember thinking "but this is so bad this will never happen," but I was so glad that, especially when sales were slow in the beginning, that we did go for the worst case scenario, because that's really when it sort of happens and that definitely helps you, when business is slow, to actually raise enough money for it and warn the bank manager, because the last thing you want is some bank manager breathing down your neck.

In 2001 we had a turnover of £30 million and we were on the main stock exchange valued at £50million and everyone sort of told us that this is the time of the exit, and so we both sold our shares at that point, but it was really only the following day after selling our shares, and resigning from the positions we had, that I realized what a terrible mistake we had made and how much I loved this company I started, and how an entrepreneur should never really sell their companies without thinking twice about it. But when you do something you love, why should you take that away from your life? Why would you ever do that?

WHAT HAVE YOU BEEN UP TO SINCE YOU SOLD THE BUSINESS?

I've written two books – 'Anyone Can Do It' and 'Switched On' and I've also started another business 'Skinny Candy' but I love passing on the lessons I learnt from when companies get big how you mustn't lose the entrepreneurial spirit that got you there in the first place. What I do now is speak to big companies about how to keep their entrepreneurial spirit alive.

WHAT IS SUCCESS?

For me, success is loving what you do and so that when you get up, work doesn't feel like work, and I believe that work is a great part of your life but you have to make sure it's something you love, and something you love by definition, and something you're good at as well, so true success is when you're doing something you love that makes you money that, as you know, gives you remuneration and financial rewards also, but it's the balance between both. I think that really is the definition of success and every morning you look forward to getting up and almost sort of can't wait to go to work and a Monday morning doesn't feel like a cliché Monday morning to you.

WHAT IS HAPPINESS?

Defining happiness is difficult for me. I would say happiness is feeling in the flow - doing something you enjoy that is challenging, that you feel you are good at, and that you have a nice balance and a bit of both. And also that you are interested and curious. That you are on a journey, I suppose, that is what happiness is. The opposite of happiness, for me, is slight boredom. So I'm happiest when I'm stimulated, and be that what I do at work or be that gardening or with my pets or with my family and friends. It comes in different shapes and sizes depending on what sort of mood you are in.

WHAT ONE PIECE OF ADVICE WOULD YOU GIVE AND ASPIRING ENTREPRENEUR?

The one piece of advice I would give to an aspiring entrepreneur would be that anyone can do it. Entrepreneurship is... if you have an idea, just the steps you take that turn you into an entrepreneur, so never think twice about whether or not you are an entrepreneur, just think about your idea and step by step go through the steps you need to carry out your idea and you become an entrepreneur. It's not an easy journey but it's an absolutely wonderful journey of discovery and it's definitely worth it!

SUCCESS IS LOVING WHAT YOU DO SO THAT WHEN YOU GET UP, WORK DOESN'T FEEL LIKE WORK

CASE STUDY

ADAM SOPHER, JOE & SEPHS

THE ONLY INVESTMENT WAS THE POTS AND PANS, AND A FEW HOURS IN KITCHEN

WHAT WAS YOUR LIGHT BULB MOMENT IN COMING UP WITH YOUR BUSINESS?

So the idea for Joe & Sephs came from my dad, Joseph and his recipes for popcorn that he made us as kids for years and years. It was just his hobby to make great tasting popcorn and he used all sorts of different ingredients all natural. Big whole pieces of corn, as opposed to often those little broken bits that you get to make this amazing tasting popcorn and for years we wondered why no one else in the UK did anything and there was only one large brand at the time that dominated the popcorn world and in 2010 my mum and dad had retired and I was a bit bored in the job that I was doing so we thought let's have a go and see what people think of it. We took the popcorn to BBC food show at Olympia and in 2010 and we had no idea if it was going to be a success or not but on the way there we actually called a local hospital to see whether or not they would like to take the entire car load of popcorn that we had with us at the time in case we didn't sell any. Fortunately though the show was a great success and we sold out in two days made such a scene at the show for the queue of people at the stand a Selfridges buyer actually saw us at the show and decided to list us just 5 months later. That was our very first retail listing.

HOW DID YOU COME UP WITH THE NAME?

The name joe and sephs is literally my dads name, Joseph, split into two. We split the joe from the seph and misspelt it a little bit, the reason it's his name is that he is our chef and he's the one that created all the diff recipes of the popcorn and also my mums name is Jacqui and joe and Jacqui or my name joe and adams are not very good. Joes popcorn sounds too American and being such a British brand was really important.

HOW DID YOU RAISE FINANCE?

So we really started Joe & Sephs with a relatively small amount of money, the initial investment was in creating our logo our website and coming up with some packaging ideas, and we did it that on less than 10k including our first trade show stand and everything. That came out of savings and an overdraft we managed to secure with National West bank at the time. There was no need to build a factory or spend huge amounts of money. The initial production runs were done in a rent by the hour kitchen and we spent the bare minimum amounts of money as possible. You would then go into this kitchen, clean it, cook, clean it again, and so the only investment there was pots and pans, and few hours in kitchen. It was really started on an absolute shoe string. Then as we secured more and more listings and we needed to scale and take on bigger premises, it has always been that delicate art of balancing cash flow but we have never taken external investment, it has just been funding through overdrafts banks.

WHAT WAS THE BIGGEST CHALLENGE YOU FACED WHEN STARTING UP?

The biggest challenges we have faced is around our cash flow, and just the good problem of growing a business that is growing so fast and, because we produce the product ourselves, not just scaling the marketing and sales teams but scaling production premises and production team and packaging machinery too. So cash flow is something every small business faces and there are some retailers that are notorious with dreadful payment terms as well. So it has been a delicate balancing act but we have taken on the right business at the right time so to mean that we have never really had too much of a challenge on it. The scalability challenge is a good problem, is a big challenge and just about making sure that you walk before you can run and that you don't take on massive contracts without having the capacity to be able to deal with them. Sometimes that may sway the growth a little bit but at least that means you don't let down any customers. Meaning you build a large and sustainable business.

WHAT IS SUCCESS?

Success for me is two fold I guess. So I want to build a brand that is long lasting, and known for producing fantastic, unique and innovative and really tasty products and so that success will be for me when I can look back on it in 10 years time and see that those principles are still there and that business is still thriving on the back of producing great tasting, premium, quality products. The other element which is kind of linked to that, is the success I feel from growing our team. We started as 3 family members and are now a team of 38 fantastic people who all believe passionately in what we do and have grown their own skill set and experience from working with us and the kick that both myself and parents get from all those different members of the team working so hard day in and day out is fantastic and yeah that is a real element of success. The pride we get is from our team.

WHAT IS HAPPINESS?

Happiness for me is the feedback we get from customers, some of the letters, emails and phone calls are just incredible. We have people that have suffered from anorexia and haven't been able to eat and written us emails saying that it was our popcorn that reminded them how amazing food can be and it got them to eat again. We have letters from customers who have eaten our popcorn whilst watching a movie and have proposed to watching that movie and endless emotional stories and I love the thought of tens of thousands of people out there eating our products in such unique situations and hopefully all of them enjoying it and having different experiences and I get an absolute kick out of people eating our popcorn and enjoying it and seeing how something you have worked so hard for has developed so much and other people are enjoying it so much as well.

WHAT ONE PIECE OF ADVICE WOULD YOU GIVE AN ASPIRING ENTREPRENEUR?

The one bit of advice I would offer to anyone who is aspiring to become an entrepreneur is to talk to people and to network. It is amazing how giving of their time people can be. Myself I have spoken to so many people in the industry over the course of the last 5 years of when we were just thinking of starting to growing the business quite substantially over the past few years, and asking people in the industry who have done a similar thing what mistakes they have made and what opportunities they have had and challenges they have faced and actually from having those conversations you can walk away with quite a clear head about what it is you are wanting to be doing. And the next steps that you have to make to get there. It's great to be able to go to people and ask for their advice and definitely networking and having some good conversations with fascinating people is something I would recommended everyone to do.

> I GET AN **ABSOLUTE KICK** OUT OF PEOPLE EATING OUR POPCORN AND ENJOYING IT... SEEING HOW SOMETHING YOU HAVE WORKED SO HARD FOR HAS DEVELOPED.

CASE STUDY

PETER GRAINGER, CAFE POD

DEALING WITH THE UPS AND DOWNS AND HOW TO TAKE THE PUNCHES AND KEEP MOVING FORWARD

WHAT WAS YOUR LIGHT BULB MOMENT IN COMING UP WITH YOUR BUSINESS?

It was kind of being in the right place at the right time. I finished up a job in the city as a travelling caddy and then spent 8 months in Morocco to clear my head and wait for the next chapter . I just saw somebody making their own capsules and selling them. After a small chat, I was amazed at the money he was making. We were having this conversation about a whole new category and I was like, actually I'm discovering, slowly enough, to do something about it . That was in cape town 2011 and then I started.

WHEN YOU MET AND SPOKE TO THE GUY THAT WAS DOING IT, WAS IT PRETTY MUCH DURING THAT CONVERSATION WHEN YOU WERE LIKE I WANT TO DO THAT TOO?

Yeah I went in there to buy capsules from him, and he was making them himself when I went to buy them, and he said how he wants to sell into the UK. My first instinct was to sell them online when I came back, but I spoke to Brent and he said we'd create more value if we can make them ourselves.

WHY DID YOU NAME IT CAFÉ POD?

We were thinking about coffee caps, coffee capsules, coffee pods and we were checking online what was available. Café pod was available so we registered the company under this name. It was never supposed to be the branding because we actually set up the company to be a manufacturer for other companies. We knew there was going to be a demand for production. When we realized that nobody wanted production but brands, we would have to go and create a brand. When we went to see an agency they said it's pretty catchy, why just not stick with that? And that's what we did!

HOW DID YOU RAISE FINANCE?

In the beginning we had pretty much no money. We knew if we wanted to do anything we have to manufacture it by ourselves instead of importing it from South Africa. The guy in Cape Town along with one or two other people were the only people in the world who manufactured it. So we knew we had to buy equipment to manufacture. That was half a million pounds. So we knew we wouldn't get off the ground unless we raised finance. It wasn't should we or shouldn't we. It was we have to. We were all working at the time and we used to meet up in the evenings. We knew if we wanted to raise money, first we needed a business plan. So we spent ages putting together financial projections and what the market is going to be like and how we are going to grow the market. After that we drew up a list of people we wanted to talk to and started hiring. We did meetings and met with probably hundreds of people. We managed to raise 750,000 pounds to be able to get a deposit down for a machine.

WHAT WAS THE BIGGEST CHALLENGE WHEN YOU WERE STARTING IT UP?

We just knew nothing. Which is exciting but we also literally had no base knowledge on anything. We started everything from scratch. There were so many things to do, because we were going into an industry that was brand new. We were creating the category in the UK. You could not buy any espresso capsules in the supermarkets. The supermarkets didn't know what to make of this. We have never made a food product before, we didn't know anything about what branding was. The funny thing is getting the product on the shelf, is normally the difficult part, but was actually easier. We were dealing with the unknown and every day something would happen we didn't foresee. Dealing with the ups and downs and how to take the punches and keep moving forward and not emotionally react to things – it was pretty tough. It's definitely not glamorous… especially in the beginning.

WHEN APPROACHING PEOPLE FOR INVESTMENTS, DID ANYONE SAY: "WHY ARE YOU DOING THIS? YOU HAVE GOT NO EXPERIENCE, NO KNOWLEDGE"?

Most people literally were like that's ridiculous. I think half of the people didn't even really understand what we were trying to do. A lot of people we had talked to had a Nespresso machine. Nespresso is owned by Nestlé. It is the world's biggest food company. Nespresso is the jewel on their crown. And you want to go and attack that. They were like you are crazy, this is ridiculous. And you have no experience in any of this, you have never done this before. Yeah, so a lot of people were like get out. Not in a bad way but it was just like "Good luck guys. You were all in decent jobs before. I hope you know what you are doing."

DID YOU STOP BY GOING IN WITH THE ASSUMPTION THAT YOU WOULD HAVE TO FACE THOSE CHALLENGES OR DID YOU DEVELOP A MINDSET GOING WE ARE GOING TO JUSTIFY WHY THIS IS DOABLE?

You have always got to give it a go. You need to be like this is going to be amazing and we are going to smash this and this is going to be a success. Anything less than that and people do not get blown over. So we were very single-minded. We didn't understand why people didn't see the billion-dollar picture. This industry is massive. We are the first people in this country to do it. We were the first in the world. We are in such a great position, why is anybody even questioning? We saw the big picture so crystal clear and it didn't really matter what anybody said to us. We were like if you don't want to get on this, that is your loss. We were stubborn.

WHAT MISTAKES DID YOU MAKE?

I mean, the three of us started originally and we are all friends, we all work together, we all go on holiday together. It was a challenging part of it and a great part of it. What you spend money on in the beginning, what you think is important, ends up not being important. You end up spending money on irrelevant things, which means you run out of money. Early wins that you make you don't realize are important… they are. We got listings in supermarkets and lost them. If we look back now, the business would now be in such a different position had we known how crucial it was for that not to happen. Assuming it is all going to go to the plan, that is probably the biggest mistake a business makes. Assuming you've got a plan and it's all going to go that way. I'm saying it is twice as much and twice as long. No matter how good we are at planning and forecasting. You don't know what is coming.

> YOU HAVE ALWAYS GOT TO GIVE IT A GO

DID YOU LEARN ANYTHING IN PARTICULAR FROM FINDING OUT WHAT YOU DIDN'T KNOW OR MAKING ANY MISTAKES?

We didn't understand the value of brand. We started arguing in the beginning why should we make a brand we can just make for other people, it's cheaper, it's easier, there is volume there. And we argued and debated for ages and eventually we came around to the fact maybe we should do our own brand. To the point now where we realized that the branding is everything and making it for other people is just a waste of time. And it is very short-term. That was one of the big learnings I suppose.

to be a success. Anything less than that and people do not get blown over. So we were very single-minded. We didn't understand why people didn't see the billion-dollar picture. This industry is massive. We are the first people in this country to do it. We were the first in the world. We are in such a great position, why is anybody even questioning? We saw the big picture so crystal clear and it didn't really matter what anybody said to us. We were like if you don't want to get on this, that is your loss. We were stubborn.

WHAT MISTAKES DID YOU MAKE?

I mean, the three of us started originally and we are all friends, we all work together, we all go on holiday together. It was a challenging part of it and a great part of it. What you spend money on in the beginning, what you think is important, ends up not being important. You end up spending money on irrelevant things, which means you run out of money. Early wins that you make you don't realize are important... they are. We got listings in supermarkets and lost them. If we look back now, the business would now be in such a different position had we known how crucial it was for that not to happen. Assuming it is all going to go to the plan, that is probably the biggest mistake a business makes. Assuming you've got a plan and it's all going to go that way. I'm saying it is twice as much and twice as long. No matter how good we are at planning and forecasting. You don't know what is coming.

> YOU HAVE ALWAYS GOT TO GIVE IT A GO

DID YOU LEARN ANYTHING IN PARTICULAR FROM FINDING OUT WHAT YOU DIDN'T KNOW OR MAKING ANY MISTAKES?

We didn't understand the value of brand. We started arguing in the beginning why should we make a brand we can just make for other people, it's cheaper, it's easier, there is volume there. And we argued and debated for ages and eventually we came around to the fact maybe we should do our own brand. To the point now where we realized that the branding is everything and making it for other people is just a waste of time. And it is very short-term. That was one of the big learnings I suppose.

> IT IS WHAT YOU CAN DO WITH THE SUCCESS THAT MAKES THE DIFFERENCE.

HOW MUCH EARLY ON DID YOU DISAGREE WITH?

Day one. But you need people to bring different things to the party. I am the hand-break , Brent is the accelerator. and it's a good balance. Sometimes the accelerator is needed and sometimes the break is needed depending on what challenge we are facing. In the early days it is literally a rollercoaster ride so you are trying to adapt and learning how to make decisions and learning how to make 50 decisions every day. It is tiring. Working in a role doesn't prepare you for that. Nobody is asking you because you are the only employer. You haven't got anybody who is turning around when you ask what you should do. So you are going to talk between each other and figure out which path is the right one to pick. Sometimes you are clueless.

DID YOU HAVE DIFFERENCES THAT WERE INCOMPATIBLE OR YOU HAD TO OVERCOME?

Good question. Sometimes differences can be complimentary but also if you don't understand the differences they can cause clashes. So it's like an analytical person, a creative person and the analytical person not understanding the value of creative. So you need both. If you don't understand the value the other skills bring to the party you can clash because like why are you spending all the time doing that when you need to be doing this? I think we have both become so much better at realizing the value that every single aspect in a business brings. Actually, we have learned to appreciate it and we have learned where each of our skills lie even more. I mean Brent and I had about a thousand clashes and debates and arguments.

DID YOU EVER THINK OF GIVING UP?

No, never. Brent is stubborn and very single-minded and so am I. It is funny when you read entrepreneurial books they are always like you need to understand your why, you need to have your reason, you need to understand why you are doing this. As ridiculous as that sounds, it is probably the most important thing and it cannot be money. Because there will always be an easier way to make money or something else that can make you more money. It is going to be something that is intangible that really is this burning desire inside to do. I think for Brent and I, for both of us, in a general sense it is both family driven. Recently, he got married, he has got a little daughter. He wants to make sure that they don't have to worry ever again. I am not married but I have got my mum and my brother. Mom is getting on I want to make sure she never has to worry. She gave me a lot when I was growing up in terms of support and I want to be able to repay that. I need to be in a position where I can let her enjoy the rest of her life. But in order for that to happen I need to get my shit together and I need to do something. It is what you can do with the success that makes the difference. That desire makes you very single focused because it is something that is very personal, which you need. You can't just be in it for the money.

PEOPLE SAY I DON'T REALLY CARE ABOUT MONEY, IT IS ALRIGHT, KEEP THINGS COOL. DO YOU THINK OF IT LIKE THAT? IT IS A TOOL, IT IS A WAY OF KEEP THINGS COOL?

There are a number of assets we have. It depends where your starting point is. If you have grown up with money and your are not really worrying about it then I think you come in a really different way than as if you were always scraping together and you have never really been comfortable. My family did not have a lot of money growing up, so it has always been a challenge getting the bills paid or being able to pay for things. Money doesn't buy happiness, it buys you options. It is the option of what you can do in your life or not do which is important. It is competitiveness with yourself or with each other. It is like running a marathon or triathlon. You first want to see if you can finish it. Then you are like, oh can I beat my previous time, can I do better on the run. It becomes just about being better and growing. You are maybe the best in the world or one millionth in the world. You still achieved what you perceived as your grades or being the best you can be. When you start being confident in your skills and your abilities and can build up a £100 million company, I have the skills, let me see if I can actually do it, it becomes a task like I can run a three-hour marathon.

DID YOU EVER FACE CASH-FLOW PROBLEMS?

Yes, today. Yesterday. All the time. The funny thing is you might have a month or two where you are not having extreme issues but you end up making your bit of money. If somebody grows like we do you end up investing in people and facilities and more development, which means you end up spending more cash because you think you will make more money. It will keep happening because the way we want to grow and be aggressive is we will always spend to very high-tolerance or low-tolerance of what we can afford, because the more money we make the more we will just invest to try and make the boat go up quicker. But I have seen people start businesses in our industry who had tons of money and the stupid mistakes they have made because they haven't had really considered. If I had a hundred pounds, what do I spend it on? I would learn from these mistakes because I have considered it. It is a balance between the lessons you learn from having money and not having money.

TAKE GEORGE LUCAS AS AN EXAMPLE. HE HAD NO MONEY AND MADE THREE AMAZING FILMS - STAR WARS - AND HE HAD ALL THE MONEY IN THE WORLD AND MADE TWO TERRIBLE FILMS. HE HAD COMPLETE CONTROL, TONS OF BUDGET AND MESSED IT UP.

Being comfortable doesn't bring the best out of people. When we start seeing we are starting to achieve things and start to get, efficient at processes, I think Brent and I automatically started creating more things to do to move us outside of the comfort zone. It keeps you on your toes because you have never done that before. Staying in the comfort zone is easy. But nothing really amazing comes from easy situations.

DO YOU EVER HAVE TO JUSTIFY YOURSELF WHEN YOUR INVESTORS OR SHAREHOLDERS DISAGREE?

People around us, whether it is friends or other companies in our field or just investors, they like what we are trying to do and they have previous experience. I don't think we have ever had a big clash with people. People trust us and invested in us that we will make the right decision. But when we need a bit of counseling and guidance we will come to the people we need to. Brent and I are assuming we know nothing and we go to people where we value their opinion.

WHAT IS SUCCESS?

I suppose standing out, achieving what you set out to achieve. You can't be disappointed if you have no expectations. Depending on how ridiculous your vision is sometimes you think there I no way to get there but even if I get halfway there, that would be amazing. I think success, for Brent and I, is for us to come up with an idea or strategy and put it down and then say yes we can do that and go and do it. At the time we didn't even know thirty percent of what we needed to know, but we found a way around, and to us that's success. Because you are building life skills and knowledge and confidence and the more that happens the more you want to be more successful. Having fun and feeling like you're engaged.

SOME PEOPLE SET UP A COMPANY AND SELL IT TO A BIG COMPANY AND DON'T WORK ANYMORE WHEN THEY ARE 45. IS THAT A PICTURE OF SUCCESS FOR YOU?

No. I'm sure if that ever comes, we probably take a couple of months off, enjoy the beach and the sun and surf. But we wouldn't even probably sit still then but look for something else to do. Building your own business keeps you stimulated every day and you constantly having to fix things and overcome things but you're using your mind in a way it is supposed to be used. If we would stop that after years and years it would be like you are doing weightlifting and never go to the gym again. Your brain will fade and your mind will fade. When you are strong you want to keep using it or build it even further. I like the sun and the beach but I'm sure ill find something else to work on myself.

WHAT IS HAPPINESS TO YOU?

Being engaged with things you enjoy. Often, phrases are used like living a full life, living in the moment and having balance, which I don't believe, exists. It is not bad doing stuff that really excites

IT IS A BALANCE BETWEEN THE LESSONS YOU LEARN FROM HAVING MONEY AND NOT HAVING MONEY.

you and engages you and uses all your potential. You have to pull out every resource that you have. London could be anywhere but I am so oblivious to the world around me because I'm so focused. The last two years, people want two things in life: meaningful relationships and meaningful work. That's the best definition of happiness. If you have those two things, you would be okay.

WERE YOU HAPPY BEFORE YOUT STARTED YOUR OWN BUSINESS?

The job I had before was in the city. I was there for about ten years, for the company I was working for about five years. It was ridiculously hard, as we were working a hundred hour week because my boss was demanding. But the whole company's ethos was we only have the best and if you are going to be here you need to be the best and need to give everything. But through that you learn a great work ethic and you are around top quality people, which means you are pushing your game all the time. The founders of that company wanted to be the best in the world at their game and they became that. Being part of that process, as tiring and is difficult it was, was fascinating. I wouldn't have been there for five years if I didn't enjoy it but I also enjoy chilling out and exploring and seeing what is around.

WHAT PIECE OF ADVICE WOULD YOU GIVE TO AN ASPIRING ENTREPRENEUR?

Don't do it for the glamour because there isn't any. In the early days execution is everything. Moving forward is everything. Getting stuff done and just making sure you are stepping forward one step at a time. Don't get caught up being cool and talking like you are a rock star. Business is about building something, making a profit, employing people, making a difference to the people who work for you and the people who buy your products. Hanging out and being cool and being a "celebrity" doesn't pay the bills.

YOU HAVE TO PULL OUT EVERY RESOURCE THAT YOU HAVE.

HOW DID YOU SCORE?

POP QUIZ ANSWERS:

1. Answer: £2.28 :
Method: £4.99/1.2= £4.15 which is the RRP net of VAT. Then 100%-45%=55%. Multiply £4.15* .55= £2.28

2. Answer: 59%
Method: a) £1.05-.43=.62 b) .62/1.05= .59 c) .59 as a percentage is 59% (.59*100)

3. Answer: £7.44.
Method: a) £4.99/ (100%-33%)= £7.44

4. Answer: The retailer buys for £2.90, the wholesaler buys for £2.18 and my margin is 33%.
Method: a) 3.49/12 = £2.90 (price net of VAT). B) 2.90*(100%-25%)= £2.18 c) £2.18 * (100%-28%)= £1.56 d) 1.56-1.05/1.56= 33%

www.ingramcontent.com/pod-product-compliance
Lightning Source LLC
Chambersburg PA
CBHW062353220526
45472CB00008B/1782